The Injustice Department

The Injustice Department

An Elected Attorney General And an Independent Department of Justice

Inprint Books

La Jolla, California

Also by Joel D. Joseph

Legal Agreements in Plain English (1982)

How to Fight City Hall . . . The IRS, Banks, Corporations, Your Local Airport & Other Nuisances (1983)

Father/Son Book (1985)

The Glove Compartment Book (1985)

Employees Rights in Plain English (1985)

Black Mondays: Worst Decisions of the Supreme Court (First Edition: 1987, Second Edition: 1989, Third Edition: 2008, Fourth Edition: 2014) (Foreword by Justice Thurgood Marshall)

Made in the USA: The Complete Guide to America's Finest Products (1990-1996)

Fifty Ways to Create Jobs in the United States (2010)

All American Holiday Gift Guide (2011)

All American Back to School Guide (2011)

Inequality in America: 10 Causes and 10 Cures

Myth of German Engineering: Cars and Products that are Unsafe, Unreliable and Expensive to Maintain (2021)

Contents

Chapter One

Introduction

"If the events of September 11, 2001, have proven anything, it's that the terrorists can attack us, but they can't take away what makes us American - our freedom, our liberty, our civil rights. No, only Attorney General John Ashcroft can do that."

--Jon Stewart

"It simply cannot be that the president can name his own temporary attorney general to supervise an investigation in which he and his family have a direct, concrete interest."

--Neal Katyal, Acting Solicitor General

'

Real Independence

Attorney General William Barr was a puppet for President Trump and not the head of an independent Department of Justice. President Trump interfered in the prosecution of his longtime associate Roger Stone by criticizing via twitter his sentencing. Trump also interfered with the sentencing of his former National Security Advisor Lieutenant General Michael Flynn. The former President interfered with several investigations being conducted by the U.S. Attorney for the Southern District of New York.

Trump tweeted that Stone's recommended seven to nine-year prison sentence as "horrible and very unfair." The Justice Department announced soon after Trump's tweet that it would seek a shorter prison term, prompting four career prosecutors to resign from the case in protest.

The Justice Department's decision to overrule its own prosecutors' sentencing recommendation was highly unusual and sparked concerns that Attorney Gen. William P. Barr, who had strongly backed Trump, was bowing to political pressure to help the president's former advisor.

Barr's interference came only four days after Trump, newly emboldened by his Senate acquittal on impeachment charges, ordered the recall of his ambassador to the European Union and the ouster of a decorated Army officer from the National Security Council as public payback for their damaging testimony during the inquiry.

On the evening of February 10, 2020, the team prosecuting Roger Stone submitted a 26-page memo in federal court recommending a sentence of seven to nine years in prison, within federal sentencing guide-lines. The memo raised the prospect that Stone, then age 67, could receive the harshest sentence of the half-dozen former Trump campaign aides and others charged in the Russia investigation.

But the next day, the Justice Department sent a revised recommendation, saying the earlier one "does not accurately reflect the Department of Justice's position on what would be a reasonable sentence in this matter" and that the actual sentence should be "far less."

The revised Justice Department memo urged U.S. District Judge Amy Berman Jackson, who was hearing the case, to consider Stone's "advanced age, health, personal circumstances, and lack of criminal history in fashioning an appropriate sentence."

The move prompted a swift response from the four prosecutors who tried the case against Roger Stone and earned a conviction. Jonathan Kravis was the first to resign, both from the case and as an assistant U.S. attorney. Soon after, Aaron Zelinsky, the lead prosecutor on the case, notified the court that he was resigning "effective immediately" as a special prosecutor with the U.S. attorney's office in Washington, but would stay on as an assistant U.S. attorney in Baltimore.

The other two federal prosecutors on the case, Adam Jed and Michael Marando, also withdrew.

These four prosecutors all had sterling credentials, including several Supreme Court clerkships.

In the entire history of the Justice Department there has never been such a brash interference with the prosecution of a case. More than 2,000 former Justice Department officials and U.S. Attorneys wrote an open letter to the Attorney General calling upon him to resign. "It is unheard of for the Department's top leaders to overrule line prosecutors, who are following established policies, in order to give preferential treatment to a close associate of the President, as Attorney General Barr did in the Stone case," the letter states. "Those actions, and the damage they have done to the Department of Justice's reputation for integrity and the rule of law, require Mr. Barr to resign."

A national association of federal judges called an emergency meeting to address growing concerns about the intervention of Justice Department officials and President Donald Trump in politically sensitive cases. Philadelphia U.S. District Judge Cynthia Rufe, who heads the independent Federal Judges Association, said the group "could not wait" until its spring conference to weigh in on a deepening crisis that has enveloped the Justice Department and Attorney General William Barr.

Special Prosecutors

We would not have needed special prosecutors like Robert Mueller, Kenneth Starr, Archibald Cox or Leon Jaworski if the Department of Justice and the Attorney General were independent of the White House.

Attorney General Jeff Sessions, who recused himself from the Russian inquiry, nonetheless assisted President Trump in his removal of James Comey as head of the FBI. Neither the Attorney General, nor President Trump, had the right to fire the FBI director.

Eighty-two years ago, the U.S. Supreme Court ruled against Franklin Roosevelt's firing of an FTC Commissioner. *Humphey's Executor v. United States*, 295 U.S. 602, 1935. The Director of the FBI, like the commissioners of the Federal Trade Commission must be independent of the president of the United States.

Director Comey, like Commissioner Humphrey, was appointed for a designated term and could only be fired for cause. The cause cited by the president was clearly subterfuge—the real reason was to stop Comey's investigation of the Trump campaign's connection with Russia. James Comey could have filed suit to challenge his termination, but apparently decided not to challenge President Trump's actions, and to publish his side of the story in his book, *A Higher Loyalty.*

Let the People Decide

Let the people decide who should enforce our laws. An independent elected Attorney General would no longer be the president's puppet, crony or brother. An independent Attorney General would appoint all of the U.S. attorneys without any political assistance from the president or senators. An independent Justice Department and an independent FBI would investigate alleged crimes committed by occupants of the White House without fear of being fired and would improve the public's level of confidence in the fairness of the legal system.

Chapter Two
The First Attorney General

The office of the Attorney General was established by the Judiciary Act of 1789 as a part-time job for one person. George Washington chose the first attorney general, Edmund Randolph, one of the lesser-known Founding Fathers. Randolph was selected as one of 11 delegates to represent Virginia at the Continental Congress in 1779 and served as a delegate through 1782. During this period he also remained in private law practice, handling numerous legal issues for George Washington and other clients.

Randolph Was a Young Founding Father

In 1776, at the age of twenty-three years, Randolph became the youngest member of the Virginia constitutional convention. He helped draft and adopt the Virginia Declaration of Rights as well as a new state constitution in 1776. In that same year Randolph married Elizabeth Nicholas, daughter of Virginia's new state treasurer. They had four children. Like many elected officials at the time, Randolph continued his private interests—running his estate and his law practice—while he was in office.

Randolph continued to advance in the political world. With a new state government formed, Randolph was appointed its first attorney general. He served for ten years, and during his tenure as Virginia attorney general he was elected mayor of Williamsburg.

Father and Son on Different Sides of Civil War

The Revolutionary War broke out on April 19, 1775 in Lexington, Massachusetts, where eight Americans were killed and a British soldier was slightly wounded. Later that day shots of the war were fired in Lexington and Concord, Massachusetts, where the first British soldiers fell.

When the Revolution broke out, Randolph and his father followed different paths. John Randolph, a Loyalist, followed the royal governor, Lord Dunmore, to England, in 1775. Edmund then lived with his uncle
Peyton Randolph, a prominent figure in Virginia politics. During the Revolutionary War Edmund served as an aide-de-camp to General Washington.

In 1779, Edmund Randolph was elected to the Continental Congress, and in November, 1786 Randolph became Governor of Virginia. In 1786, he was a delegate to the Annapolis Convention.

The Constitutional Convention

Four days after the opening of the federal convention in Philadelphia, on May 29, 1787, Edmund Randolph presented the Virginia Plan for creating a new government. This plan proposed a strong central government composed of three branches, legislative, executive, and judicial, and enabled the legislature to veto state laws and use force against states that failed to fulfill their duties. After many debates and revisions, including striking the section permitting force against a state, the Virginia Plan became in large part the basis of the Constitution.

Though Randolph introduced the highly centralized Virginia Plan, he fluctuated between the Federalist and Antifederalist points of view. He sat on the Committee of Detail that prepared a draft of the Constitution, but by the time the document was adopted, Randolph declined to sign. He felt it was not sufficiently republican, and he was especially wary of creating a one-man executive. He preferred a three-man council since he regarded "a unity in the Executive" to be the "foetus of monarchy." In a letter on the Federal Constitution, dated October 10, 1787, Randolph explained at length his objections to the Constitution. The old Articles of Confederation were inadequate, he agreed, but the proposed new plan of union contained too many flaws. Randolph was a strong advocate of the process of amendment. He feared that if the Constitution were submitted for ratification without leaving the states the opportunity to amend it, the document might be rejected and thus cut off any hope of another plan of union. However, he hoped that amendments would be permitted, and second convention called to incorporate the changes.

Randolph argued against importation of slaves and in favor of a strong central government. Randolph additionally proposed, and was supported by unanimous approval by the Convention's delegates, "that a National Judiciary be established" (Article III of the Constitution established the federal court system).

The Articles of Confederation lacked a national court system for the United States and relied solely on state courts. Randolph was also a member of the Committee of Detail which was tasked with converting the Virginia Plan's fifteen resolutions into the first draft of the Constitution. Madison was the lead author. However, when the Constitution was adopted in final form, Randolph and fellow Virginia delegate George Mason refused to sign it. They believed the Constitution did not provide sufficient protection of individual rights. They also thought the newly created position of president was too much like a monarch, holding excessive power. Randolph tried to promote the idea of a three-person executive committee rather than a single president; he also argued that the proposed single president should not be allowed to run for reelection.

Randolph was so concerned about the new Constitution that he published a letter opposing it when he returned to Virginia from the Philadelphia convention. He also recommended that the delegates hold a second convention but to no avail.

The following year, in 1788, Randolph attended the Virginia convention for ratifying the Constitution. However, Randolph chose to support its approval, joining fellow Virginia delegates Madison and Marshall. Eight other states had already ratified the Constitution at the time of the Virginia gathering. Randolph had concluded that its acceptance was inevitable and that Virginia should show in its support for the constitution. Randolph played a key role in the close vote favoring ratification. A number of Virginians were angered by Randolph's change in position concerning the Constitution.

Randolph ultimately refused to sign the final document, one of only three members who remained in the Constitutional Convention yet refused to sign (together with fellow Virginian George Mason and Elbridge Gerry of Massachusetts and of Gerrymandering fame). Randolph thought the final document lacked sufficient checks and balances, and published an account of his objections in October, 1787. Randolph had several objections to the Convention's proposal. He thought the federal judiciary would pose a threat to state courts, and he thought the Senate was too powerful and Congress's power too broad. He also objected to there being no provision for a second convention to act after the present instrument had been referred to the states.

Service as Attorney General

Washington rewarded Randolph for his support during the war by appointing him attorney general in September, 1789. He served as the first Attorney General from February 2, 1790 until January 2, 1794.

Randolph maintained precarious neutrality in the feud between Thomas Jefferson (of whom Randolph was a second cousin) and Alexander Hamilton. In President Washington's cabinet, as in the ratification dispute of 1787–1788, Randolph tried to bring people together, rather than jumping to hasty conclusions and ignoring the potential costs in pursuit of self-righteous ideological purity. He continued to make important contributions to the structure of the new nation and to its relationship with the states.

The Constitution did not establish the office of attorney general, the Justice Department or the FBI. In 1789 we were a developing nation with a small population without the need for a large legal bur-eaucracy.

The Office of the Attorney General and the Justice Department have evolved over the last 240 years. At first, the "Justice Department" had one part-time employee (Mr. Randolph). Now it has more than 100,000 employees, including the Federal Bureau of Investigation.

Not many records from Mr. Randolph's term as attorney general have survived. The following legal opinion, written by Mr. Randolph when he was attorney general is illustrative of his service.

Legal Opinion of Edmund Randolph

Randolph wrote the following legal opinion:

> [Philadelphia, ca. Aug. 1791] The question is, whether any punishment can be inflicted on persons, treating with the Indian tribes, within the limits of the United States, for lands, lying within those limits; the preemption of which is vested in the United States?
> The constitution is the basis of fœderal power.
> This power, so far as the subject of Indians is concerned, relates To the regulation of commerce with the Indian tribes.
> To the exclusive right of making treaties.

To the right of preemption in lands.

1. Even if the act, supposed in the question, were really an infraction of the right to regulate commerce, there could be no penalty, unless the law prescribed it.

Accordingly a law of the second session enters into such a case, but only forfeits the merchandize carried into the Indian country. No other law affects it.

2. Without an existing law, no treaty, or compact made by an individual of our nation with the sovereign of another, and not partaking of a treasonable quality, is punishable.

It seems indeed to be an assumption of the sovereignty of the United States in this respect.

But the compact being in the name of an individual, does virtually disclaim any assumption of public authority. If it be void, the United States cannot be deprived of their rights.

It may be indecent and impertinent for a citizen thus to behave. But where no law is, no crime is.

As to the right of pre-emption.

No man has a right to purchase my land from my tenant.

But if he does purchase, I cannot sue him on the supposition of damages, arising from the mere act of purchase.

Nor could the United States sue the purchaser of the right of preemption, since the purchase itself is void, and their interest cannot be prejudiced by any purchase, which an individual can make.

Far less would the purchaser be indictable.

But it undoubtedly is in the power of congress, to regulate commerce with the Indians in any manner to guard the right of making treaties, by forbidding the citizens to meddle under a penalty, and to provide a security to their preemption by passing adequate laws.

Until this shall be done, I conceive that this commerce is protected by no law, but the act above mentioned; that an interference in the article of treaties has no penalty, denounced against it; and that the federal property, like that of individuals, must depend upon existing laws.

It may perhaps be proper, if the testimony be strong, to warn all persons by proclamation that the rights of government will be inforced; and pos-

sibly a monitory message to the Indians
might have a good affect.

Edm: Randolph It seems likely that
Randolph drafted this opinion in re-
sponse to the efforts made by Zachariah
Cox and his associates in the Tennessee

Yazoo Company in the spring and
summer of 1791 to create a settlement at
Muscle Shoals. Thomas Jefferson expressed concern about Cox's activities to the
governor of the Southwest Territory in
August 1791, and Washington echoed
this concern in a letter to Randolph
written two months later, laying special
emphasis on the opposition of various
Southwestern tribes to Cox's scheme
(Jefferson to William Blount, 12 Aug.
1791; Washington to Randolph, 10 Oct.
1791, Fitzpatrick, *Writings*, xxxi, 386–7).

Jefferson probably asked Randolph for an opinion
on the legal ramifications of Cox's actions at about the
same time that he wrote to Governor Blount, which
means that the opinion itself could have been written
at any time after August 12th, but before September 2,
1791, the date Jefferson left Philadelphia for Mon-
ticello. The law of the second session was the July 22,
1790 act of Congress regulating trade and intercourse
with the Indians (Annals, ii, 2301–3).

Randolph spent many of the next several years trying to ease the growing split between Secretary of the Treasury Alexander

Hamilton (1755–1804) and Secretary of State Thomas Jefferson (1743– 1826). Hamilton and Jefferson represented different political factions that disagreed over economic and foreign policies. The political division widened after France declared war on Britain in early 1793. Some

American political leaders wanted to support France; others preferred Britain. With Randolph's support, President Washington chose a position of neutrality (not favoring either warring party) in the spring of 1793. President Washington sent Supreme Court Chief Justice John Jay (1745– 1829) to Britain in the summer of 1794 to negotiate a new treaty.

On November 19, 1794 the United States and Great Britain signed Jay's Treaty, which sought to settle outstanding issues between the two countries that had been left unresolved since American independence.

Randolph was the attorney general until January 2, 1794 when he was appointed Secretary of State, replacing Thomas Jefferson as Secretary of State

Randolph objected to a Supreme Court Justice negotiating a treaty. He believed a Supreme Court justice should not be involved in executive office business, and he urged keeping a sharp separation between the branches of government. Randolph thought Jay should at least resign from the Court, but

Jay did not. Nonetheless, with assistance from Hamilton, Randolph drew up instructions for Jay to follow in negotiating with Britain and asked him specifically to negotiate a new trade agreement. However, because of Hamilton's continued meddling and the length of time needed for communication across the Atlantic Ocean, Jay did not follow Randolph's guidance very closely.

Disappointed with the results of Jay's negotiations, Randolph advised President Washington not to sign the treaty. His advice attracted strong criticism from Hamilton and others who supported adoption of the new treaty by Jay. Nonetheless, the Senate ratified the Jay Treaty while

Randolph was Secretary of State. Jay's Treaty was immensely unpopular with the American public, but it squeaked through the Senate on a 20 to 10 vote on June 24, 1795, meeting the Constitution's two-thirds requirement without a vote to spare.

When the French learned of the treaty, they strongly protested. French political leaders claimed that by signing the treaty the United States had violated its 1778 alliance agreement with France. Randolph denied this was the case. The new treaty did set the stage for negotiations for a new treaty with Spain to secure navigation rights for Americans on the Mississippi River. These negotiations proved very successful and resulted in the signing of the Treaty of San Lorenzo in October, 1795.

In an effort to embarrass Randolph, the British intercepted a message from Jean Antoine Joseph Fauchet, France's minister to the United States, to Randolph that gave the appearance that Randolph was secretly dealing with Fauchet. The British then accused Randolph of influencing policy favorable to France in exchange for personal financial payments. President Washington summoned Randolph to his office to answer the charges. Humiliated, Randolph angrily resigned as Secretary of State on August 20, 1795. Fauchet denied any such dealings, and Randolph immediately wrote and published a long defense of his actions and revealed the British plot to embarrass him. No wrongdoing on Randolph's part was ever uncovered. Fauchet may have bragged to his superiors in France that he was winning favors, when in fact Randolph had not cooperated with him.

Life After Government

Randolph returned to a very successful private law practice in Richmond, Virginia. In 1807, he successfully represented former vice president Aaron Burr (1756–1836).

The Burr conspiracy was a suspected treasonous cabal of U.S. planters, politicians, and army officers in the early 19th century. The alleged conspiracy was led by Aaron Burr, the former Vice President of the United States (1801–1805). According to the accusations against him, his goal was to create an independent country in the center of North America including the Southwestern United States and parts of Mexico. Burr's version was that he intended to farm 40,000 acres in the Texas Territory which had been leased to him by the Spanish Crown.

President Thomas Jefferson ordered Burr arrested and indicted for treason, despite a lack of firm evidence. Burr's true intentions remain unclear to historians; some claim that he intended to take parts of Texas and the Louisiana Purchase for himself, others, that he intended to conquer Mexico, and yet others, that he planned to conquer most of the North American continent. The number of men backing him is also unclear, with accounts varying from fewer than forty to over seven thousand.

Burr was being tried for treason before Supreme Court chief justice John Marshall in the U.S. Circuit Court in Richmond. Burr was found not guilty. He was acquitted of treason, but the trial destroyed his already faltering political career.

After Thomas Jefferson resigned as Secretary of State, Randolph assumed that post for the years 1794-95. During the Jefferson-Hamilton conflict he tried to remain unaligned. After retiring from politics in 1795, Randolph resumed his law practice and was regarded as a leading figure in the legal community. During his retirement he wrote a history of Virginia.

When Aaron Burr went on trial for treason in 1807, Edmund Randolph acted as his senior counsel.

In 1813, at age 60 and suffering from paralysis, Randolph died while visiting Nathaniel Burwell at Carter Hall. His body is buried in the graveyard of the nearby chapel.

Legacy

The "Edmund J. Randolph Award" is the highest award given by the United States Department of Justice to persons who make "outstanding contributions to the accomplishments of the Department's mission." Randolph certainly is unique among our attorneys general. They don't make them like they used to. None of our recent attorneys general had the respect the Randolph had as one of our founding fathers. There was no need to have an elected attorney general in 1789. There really was no Justice Department then. The United States was a small, developing nation, with a small executive branch.

Neither John Mitchell, nor Eric Holder, nor William Barr had the gravitas, or even independence, of Edmund Randolph. Randolph always spoke his mind, even when he believed that the proposed Constitution was not good enough.

Chapter 3

Special Prosecutors

Archibald Cox, Leon Jaworsky,

Kenneth Starr and Robert Mueller

Special counsels have been appointed many times in our history when the President of the United States has been investigated for possible illegal activity. If we replace our politically-appointed attorney general with an independently elected attorney general, appointment of special counsels would usually be unnecessary.

The history of special counsels demonstrates how fragile our system is. President Nixon fired the special counsel investigating him and President Trump threatened to do so. We need to develop a permanent solution to the problem of investigations of the president of the United States.

Archibald Cox

Archibald Cox was Senator John F. Kennedy's labor advisor and in 1961, President Kennedy appointed him solicitor general, an office he held for four and a half years. The solicitor general argues all cases on behalf of the United States before the U.S. Supreme Court and is third in line in the Justice Department.

Cox became famous when, under mounting pressure and charges of corruption against persons closely associated with Richard Nixon,

Attorney General nominee Elliot Richardson appointed him to be Special Prosecutor to oversee the federal criminal investigation into the Watergate burglary and other related crimes that became popularly known as the Watergate scandal. Cox was at Berkeley on May 16, 1973, when Secretary of Defense Elliot Richardson, President Nixon's nominee for attorney general, called him to ask if he would consider taking the position of Special Prosecutor in the Watergate affair.

President Nixon publicly welcomed the selection and, consistent with his new public relations offensive, commended Richardson's

"determination" to get to the bottom of the affair. Privately, Nixon seethed with anger. In his memoir he said: "If Richardson searched specifically for the man whom I least trusted, he could hardly have done better."

After he was sworn in on May 25, 1973, Cox returned to Cambridge where he recruited two professors, James Vorenberg and Philip Heymann, to join his staff. The three arrived in Washington on May 29.

Cox concluded that a top priority was to hire a pre-eminent criminal trial attorney to supervise the prosecutors until the office was up and running and then try the cases after indictment. He persuaded James F. Neal, the U.S. attorney who obtained the conviction of Jimmy Hoffa in 1964 for jury tampering, then in private practice, to come aboard for several weeks to stabilize the ship. Neal however, would stay to the end. James Neal headed the largest group, the Watergate task force, which dealt with the cover up and included George Frampton, Richard BenVeniste and Jill Wine Volner.

Herb Kalmbach, personal attorney to Richard Nixon, especially of interest to the illegal campaign contributions task force, was scheduled to testify before the Senate Watergate Committee on July 16th. Instead, H.R. Haldeman, chief of staff to the Nixon Whitehouse chose his aide Col. Alexander Butterfield as a surprise witness. During his 30-minute testimony Butterfield revealed the secret taping system that was installed in the Oval Office, the president's office at the Executive Office Building, and at Camp David—a voice-activated mechanism designed to capture everything spoken by or to the president. The existence of the tapes was a blockbuster revelation unearthed by the Senate Watergate Committee

On July 23, 1973, Cox had a grand jury subpoena demanding the eight tapes and three other items served on Fred Buzhardt, counsel for Nixon. On July

26, Chief Judge John J. Sirica received a letter from Nixon himself responding to the subpoena in which he asserted that it would be as inappropriate for the court to compel him as it would for him to compel the court. He was therefore not producing the tapes. But he included a copy of the March 30 memo concerning Hunt's employment and promised to make available the Strachan political documents concerning ambassadorships. Within an hour Cox was before the grand jury, explaining the response to them. The grand jury voted to request Sirica to issue an order to Nixon to show cause why there should not be prompt compliance with the subpoena. Sirica had the members of the grand jury individually polled and issued the order.

Nixon had lost patience with Archibald Cox and was in no mood to negotiate (even though the court's suggestion strongly implied that it would order production of the tapes if there was no settlement). While his lawyers engaged in delay, Nixon was trying to control Cox through

Attorney General Richardson

For three months, Alexander Haig, H.R. Haldeman's replacement as White House chief of staff, had been directing Richardson to clamp down on Cox with increasingly more explicit threats until it reached the boiling point.

Nixon's White House counsel Fred Buzhardt nevertheless made an offer: he would summarize the tapes with each participant's conversations re-written in the third person. It was an unworkable scheme, but Cox decided to continue negotiations over the next several days. Cox then drafted a six-page counterproposal providing for transcriptions of the actual conversations together with a third-party certification that the rest of the tape was irrelevant. At the last meeting, when Nixon's lawyers showed willingness to have a third party certify transcripts, Cox gave them his proposal and then left to give them a chance to consider it. In less than an hour Buzhardt called, rejecting the proposal and ending the negotiations. The parties informed the court that they could not reach agreement.

The White House decided to fire Cox. It was unable, however, to make either Richardson or his deputy William Ruckelshaus carry out the order. Each resigned in turn rather than fire Archibald Cox, although the White House later claimed it fired Ruckelshaus. Solicitor General Robert Bork (third in line at the Justice Department) in a face-to-face meeting with the president agreed to issue the order as the acting attorney general and he also decided not to resign after terminating Cox. As for the termination itself, Bork sent a written order to Cox by messenger that evening to Cox's home.

Leon Jaworski

Under extreme criticism for firing Cox, Nixon appointed Leon Jaworski to replace him. Jaworski subsequently subpoenaed sixty-four taped conversations. On May 20, 1974, Judge Sirica ordered President Nixon to produce all sixty-four tapes to Jaworski by May 31st.

Nixon appealed on two grounds: first, that the office of Special Prosecutor did not have the right to sue the office of President; and second, that the requested materials were privileged presidential conversations. Aware that an important constitutional issue was at stake, and unwilling to wait any longer, Jaworski asked the Supreme Court to take the case directly, bypassing the Court of Appeals.

On July 24, 1974, the United States Supreme Court ruled that the Special Prosecutor did have the right to sue the President and that the "generalized assertion of [executive] privilege must yield to the demonstrated, specific need for evidence in a pending criminal trial." *United States v. Nixon*, 418 U.S. 683 (1974).

Nixon was forced to give the unedited tapes to Jaworski, including the so-called "Smoking Gun Tape" which included a compromising discussion of June 23, 1972. On August 5, 1974, the White House released this previously unknown recording. Taped only a few days after the Watergate break-in, it proved that Nixon and then-Chief of Staff H. R. Haldeman had tried to get the CIA to falsely claim national security was involved in the Watergate manner in an effort to get the FBI to end its nascent investigation.

Republicans in the Senate nominated an elder statesman to deliver to Nixon the news that he could no longer avoid impeachment in the House and conviction in the Senate. Sen. Barry Goldwater (R) of Arizona had himself been a losing presidential candidate. Goldwater had great stature in the party and would tell Nixon what he thought—that he himself would now vote for conviction. The White House agreed to a meeting late Wednesday afternoon.

Senate Republican Leader Hugh Scott, entered the Oval Office around 5 p.m. The Arizona senator sat directly in front of Nixon's desk, the others to the side. Goldwater told Nixon he had perhaps 16 to 18 Senate supporters left – too few to avoid ouster. Congressman Rhodes said House support was just as soft.

"I've got a very difficult decision to make," said Nixon, in Woodward and Bernstein's account.

No one really knows the moment Nixon decided to quit. But in the annals of Watergate this was certainly a moment of truth. Nixon later held that at this point he recognized the inevitability of resignation but was determined to not appear to have been pushed out by anyone—staff, lawmakers, or the media. Nixon **resigned the presidency on August 9, 1974.**

In the summer of 1982, seven members of the grand jury choose to break their oath of silence because "they [were] convinced justice was not done" and discussed their 30-month service with the ABC news show *20/20*. They stated they wanted to bring an indictment against President Nixon after hearing the batch of tapes released the Summer of 1974. One grand juror stated that in a straw vote, "There were 19 people in the grand-jury room that particular day, and we all raised our hands about wanting an indictment—all of us. And some of us raised both hands."

However, Jaworski did not favor an indictment, even going so far as saying he would not sign one. In discussions with the grand jury, Jaworski cited "the trauma of the country," and prior to Nixon's resignation, the lack of precedent for indicting a sitting president.

Kenneth Starr

In August, 1994, pursuant to the newly reauthorized Ethics in Government Act (28 U.S.C. § 593(b)), Kenneth Starr was appointed by a special three-judge panel of the D.C. Circuit to continue the Whitewater investigation. He replaced Robert B. Fiske, a moderate Republican who had been appointed by attorney general Janet Reno.

The Whitewater scandal was an American political controversy during the

1990s concerning the real estate investments of Bill and Hillary

Clinton and their associates, Jim McDougal and Susan McDougal, in the Whitewater Development Corporation. This failed business venture was incurporated in 1979 with the purpose of developing vacation properties on land along the White River near Flippin, Arkansas. The development was to be in the Ozarks near the South Shore of Bull Shoals Lake between the White River and the Buffalo National River 140 due north of Little Rock.

A March, 1992 *New York Times* article published during the 1992 U.S. presidential campaign reported that the Clintons, then governor and first lady of Arkansas, had invested and lost money in the Whitewater Development Corporation.

David Hale, the source of criminal allegations against the Clintons, claimed in November, 1993 that Bill Clinton had pressured him into providing an illegal $300,000 loan to Susan McDougal, the Clintons' partner in the Whitewater land deal.

The U.S. Securities and Exchange Commission had a team look into the details of the the transactions involved in Whitewater and its investigation culminated in convictions against the McDougals for their role in the Whitewater project. Jim Guy Tucker, Bill Clinton's successor as governor, was convicted of fraud and sentenced to four years of probation for his role in the matter. Susan McDougal served 18 months in prison for contempt of court for refusing to answer questions relating to Whitewater.

Kenneth Starr took the special counsel position part-time and remained active with his law firm, Kirkland & Ellis, as this was then permitted by law. As time went on, however, Starr was increasingly criticized for alleged conflicts of interest stemming from his continuing association with Kirkland & Ellis. Kirkland, like several other major law firms, was representing clients in litigation with the government, including tobacco companies and auto manufacturers. The firm itself was being sued by the Resolution Trust Company, a government agency involved in the Whitewater matter.

Starr's investigation expanded beyond the Whitewater controversy. Vince Foster, and aid President Clinton, died, either by suicide or murder on July 20, 1993.

On October 10, 1997, Starr's report on the death of deputy White House counsel Vince Foster was released to the public. The 137-page report was drafted largely by Starr's deputy Brett Kavanaugh, now a U.S. Supreme Court Justice. The report agreed with the findings of previous independent counsel Robert B. Fiske that Foster committed suicide at Fort Marcy Park, in Virginia, and that his suicide was caused primarily by undiagnosed and untreated depression.

The law conferred broad investigative powers on Starr and the other independent counsels named to investigate the administration, including the right to subpoena nearly anyone who might have information relevant to the investigation. Starr would later received express authority to conduct additional investigations, including the firing of White House Travel Office personnel, potential political abuse of confidential FBI files, Madison Guaranty, Rose Law Firm, Paula Jones lawsuit and, most notoriously, possible perjury and obstruction of justice to cover up President Clinton's sexual relationship with Monica Lewinsky.

The Lewinsky portion of the investigation included the secret taping of conversations between Lewinsky and coworker Linda Tripp, requests by Starr to tape Lewinsky's conversations with Clinton, and requests by Starr to compel Secret Service agents to testify about what they might have seen while guarding Clinton.

In his deposition for the Paula Jones civil lawsuit, President Clinton denied having "sexual relations" with Monica Lewinsky. On the basis of the evidence provided by Monica Lewinsky, a blue dress with President Clinton's semen in it, Ken Starr concluded that this sworn testimony was false and perjurious.

During the deposition in the Jones case, Clinton was asked, "Have you ever had sexual relations with Monica Lewinsky?" The judge ordered that Clinton be given an opportunity to review the agreed definition.

Clinton flatly denied having sexual relations with Lewinsky. Later, at the Starr grand jury, Clinton stated that he believed the definition of "sexual relations" agreed upon for the Jones deposition excluded his receiving oral sex.

Kenneth Starr's investigation eventually led to the impeachment of President Clinton, with whom Starr shared *Time Magazine*'s Man of the Year designation for 1998. Despite his impeachment, the president was acquitted in the subsequent trial before the United States Senate as all 45 Democrats and 10 Republicans voted to acquit him.

Robert Mueller

On May 9, 2017, President Donald Trump fired James Comey, the Director of the Federal Bureau of Investigation, who had been leading an ongoing Federal Bureau of Investigation investigation into links between Trump associates and Russian officials. This investigation, codenamed Crossfire Hurricane, began in July, 2016 after the Australian government advised U.S. authorities that George Papadopoulos, a foreign policy advisor in the Trump campaign, had met with one of their diplomats and "suggested the Trump team had received some kind of suggestion from Russia" that Russia could release information that would be damaging to Hillary Clinton. On May 10, 2016, at London's Kensington Wine Rooms, George Papadopoulos told the Australian High Commissioner to the United Kingdom, Alexander

Downer, that Russia was in possession of emails relating to Hillary Clinton.

Mr. Papadopolous had received this suggestion in Ap-ril, 2016, well before it was publicly reported that Russia had damaging information about Hillary Clinton. Papadopoulos later testified that this "damaging information" was in the form of hacked emails that were stolen from the Democratic Party.

Between March and September 2016, George Papadopoulos made at least six requests for Trump or representatives of his campaign to meet in Russia with Russian politicians. On July 27, 2017, Papadopoulos was arrested upon landing at Washington-Dulles International Airport, placed in handcuffs and leg shackles, and put in a prison cell overnight for his arraignment the following day. He was released without bail.

On September 7, 2018, George Papadopoulos was sentenced to 14 days in prison, 12 months of supervised release, 200 hours of community service and was fined $9,500. He began serving his 14-day sentence on November 26, 2018.

Over 130 Democratic lawmakers of the United States Congress called for a special counsel to be appointed in reaction to Comey's firing in 2017. CNN reported that within eight days of Comey's dismissal, an FBI investigation on Trump for obstruction of justice was opened by acting FBI Director, Andrew

McCabe, who cited multiple reasons including Comey's firing.

Eight days after Comey's dismissal, Deputy Attorney General Rod Rosenstein appointed Robert Mueller, under *28 CFR § 600.1*, as special counsel to take over and expand the existing FBI counter-intelligence investigation into possible Russian interference in the 2016 United States elections, as well as the FBI investigation into links between Trump associates and Russian officials that Comey was leading. The special counsel also took over the FBI investigation into whether President Trump obstructed justice with Comey. Rosenstein's authority to appoint Mueller arose because Attorney General Jeff Sessions recused himself from investigations into the Trump campaign because he worked for the campaign and had an apparent conflict of interest.

Upon learning that Bob Mueller had been appointed as Special Counsel, Trump said "Oh my God. This is terrible. This is the end of my presidency. I'm fucked," to Jeff Sessions when they were having a meeting in the Oval Office. "You were supposed to protect me," Sessions recalled Trump telling him. "Everyone tells me if you get one of these independent counsels it ruins your presidency. It takes years and years and I won't be able to do anything. This is the worst thing that ever happened to me," Trump later said, according to Sessions and Jody Hunt, Sessions' then chief of staff. The attorney general is supposed to protect the country, not the president of the United States.

Mueller's appointment to conduct the investigation garnered widespread support from both Democrats and Republicans in Congress.

Newt Gingrich, former Republican Speaker of the House of Representatives and prominent conservative political commentator, stated via Twitter that, "Robert Mueller is a superb choice to be special counsel. His reputation is impeccable for honesty and integrity."

Senator Charles Schumer (D-NY) said, "Former Director Mueller is exactly the right kind of individual for this job. I now have significantly greater confidence that the investigation will follow the facts wherever they lead." Senator Rob Portman (R-OH) stated, "former FBI director Mueller is well qualified to oversee this probe"

On October 30, 2017, Mueller filed charges against former Trump campaign chairman Paul Manafort and campaign co-chairman Rick Gates. The twelve charges include conspiracy to launder money, violations of the 1938 Foreign Agents Registration Act (FARA) as being an unregistered agent of a foreign principal, false and misleading FARA statements, and conspiracy against the United States. Manafort was charged with crimes in the District of Columbia and Virginia.

Paul Manafort was sentenced to 73 months in prison, with 30 months concurrent with the jail time he had received in the Virginia case, resulting in an additional 43 months in jail (30 additional months for conspiracy to defraud the United States, and 13 additional months for witness tampering). During the covid-19 pandemic, Manafort was released from prison and serving the balance of his sentence under house arrest. President Trump pardoned Manafort on December 24, 2020, just before leaving office. Trump pardoned Roger Stone at the same time.

On December 17, 2019, Rick Gates was sentenced to three years of probation, 45 days in jail, and 300 hours of community service. He was also ordered to pay a $20,000 fine. The judge took into account years of financial crimes and deception that continued even after he had agreed to plead guilty and cooperate.

Former President Trump also pardoned Gates in the last days of his administration.

On December 1, 2017, Mueller reached a plea agreement with former national security adviser Michael Flynn, who pleaded guilty to giving false testimony to the FBI about his contacts with Russian ambassador Sergey Kislyak. As part of Flynn's negotiations, his son, Michael G. Flynn, was not expected to be charged, and Flynn was prepared to testify that high-level officials on Trump's team directed him to make contact with the Russians.

Flynn was never sentenced because of many delays in his case. Attorney General Barr took over the case and moved that it be dismissed. See details in chapter ten.

On February 16, 2018, Mueller indicted 13 Russian individuals and three Russian companies for attempting to trick Americans into believing Russian propaganda that targeted Democratic nominee Hillary Clinton and later President-elect Donald Trump.

Mueller concluded his investigation on March 22, 2019 and submitted the Special Counsel's final report to Attorney General William Barr. Attorney General Barr submitted a summary of Mueller's findings to the United States Congress. He falsely stated in a letter, "The Special Counsel's investigation did not find that the Trump campaign or anyone associated with it conspired or coordinated with Russian in its efforts to influence the 2016 U.S. presidential election." Barr quoted Mueller as saying "while this report does not conclude that the President committed a crime, it also does not exonerate him."

The Department of Justice released Report on April 18, 2019 on the Investigation into Russian Interference in the 2016 Presidential Election, the special counsel's final report and its conclusions.

The *Mueller Report,* officially titled *Report on the Investigation into Russian Interference in the 2016 Presidential Election,* is the official report documenting the findings and conclusions of former Special Counsel Robert Mueller's investigation into Russian efforts to interfere in the 2016 United States presidential election, allegations of conspiracy or coordination between Donald Trump's presidential campaign and Russia, and allegations of obstruction of justice. The report was submitted to Attorney General William Barr on March 22, 2019, and a highly edited version of the 448-page report was publicly released by the Department of Justice (DOJ). It was divided into two volumes. The redactions from the report and its supporting material are under President Trump's temporary "protective assertion" of executive privilege as of May 8, 2019, preventing the material from being passed to Congress, despite earlier reassurance by Barr that Trump "confirmed" he would not exert privilege.

Volume I of the report concludes that the investigation did not find sufficient evidence that the campaign "coordinated or conspired with the Russian government in its election-interference activities."

However, the report states that Russian interference in the 2016 presidential election was illegal and occurred "in sweeping and systematic fashion" but was welcomed by the Trump campaign as it expected to benefit from such efforts. It also identifies numerous links between Trump campaign officials and individuals with ties to the Russian government, about which several persons connected to the campaign made false statements and obstructed investigations. Mueller later stated that his investigation's conclusion on Russian interference "deserves the attention of every American."

Volume II of the report addresses obstruction of justice. The investigation intentionally took an approach that could not result in a judgment that Trump committed a crime, following by an Office of Legal Counsel (OLC) opinion that a sitting president is immune from criminal prosecution.

The investigation "does not conclude that the President committed a crime" but "it also does not exonerate him."

The report describes ten episodes where Trump may have obstructed justice while president and one before he was elected, noting that he privately tried to "control the investigation." The report further states that Congress can decide whether Trump obstructed justice and take action accordingly, referencing impeachment.

On March 24, Attorney General Barr sent Congress a four-page misleading letter detailing the report's conclusions. On March 27, Mueller privately wrote to Barr, stating that the March 24 Barr letter "did not fully capture the context, nature, and substance of this office's work and conclusions" and that this led to "public confusion."

Barr declined Mueller's request to release the report's introduction and executive summaries ahead of the full report. Also on March 24, Barr's letter stated that he and for Deputy Attorney General Rod

Rosenstein concluded that the evidence was "not sufficient to establish" that Trump had obstructed justice.

In July 2019, Mueller testified before Congress that a president could be charged with crimes including obstruction of justice after they left office. In 2020, Judge Reggie Walton, a Republican-appointed federal judge decided to personally review if the report's redactions were legitimate. The judge said Barr's "misleading" statements about the report's findings led him to suspect that Barr had tried to establish a "one-sided narrative" favorable to Trump.

Conclusion

Attorney General Barr was clearly representing the interests of President Trump when he misled Congress and the American people about the content of the *Mueller Report*. Barr's unprofessional, unethical and improper handling of the *Mueller Report* demonstrates the need for an independently elected, truly independent, attorney general.

Chapter Four

Attorneys General for the States

As we elect attorneys general in nearly every state, we should elect the U.S. Attorney General. The office of Attorney General has been a political, not legal position for far too long.

An elected attorney general would be independent of the White House—he or she could not be fired by the President. The elected attorney general would be responsible to the people who elected him or her. As the FBI is part of the Justice Department, the elected attorney general would appoint the head of the Bureau.

Forty-three states elect their attorneys general, while seven states do not. Elected attorneys general serve a four-year term, except in Vermont, where the term is two year.

According to the National Association of Attorneys General, in Alaska, Hawaii, New Hampshire, New Jersey, and Wyoming, the attorney general is a gubernatorial appointee.

The attorney general in Tennessee is appointed by the Tennessee Supreme Court for an eight-year term. In Maine, the attorney general is elected by the state Legislature for a two-year term.

In addition to the states, the District of Columbia and two U.S. territories, Guam and the Northern Mariana Islands, elect their attorneys general for a four-year term In American Samoa, Puerto Rico, and the U.S. Virgin Islands, the attorney general is appointed by the governor. In Puerto Rico, the attorney general is officially called the secretary of justice, but is commonly known as the Puerto Rican attorney general.

Critically, even in states using appointment processes, the attorney general is supposed to be independent from the governor. Only Alaska and Wyoming permit the governor to remove the attorney general at will. William P. Marshall, *Break Up the Presidency? Governors, State Attorneys General, and Lessons from the Divided Executive*, 115 Yale L.J. 2446, 2448 n.3 (2006) at 2448 n.3.

Will of the People

There is strong evidence that elections prompt attorneys general to be more accountable. Elected attorneys general are more likely to shade their positions closer to the public view. While an "appointee is more likely to perceive his role . . . as a servant of state agencies," elected attorneys general are "more likely to perceive their role as the people's attorney."

William N. Thompson, *Should We Elect or Appoint State Government Executives? Some New Data Concerning State Attorneys General*, 8 Am. Rev. Pub. Admin. 17 at 41 (1974).

There is no reason that the attorney general has to be of the same party as the governor. If the electorate wants a "law and order" attorney general, they can vote for one. At the same time the electorate may want a governor to improve education, healthcare, highways, or whatever. The head of the system of justice, and the system of governing, do not have to be of the same party.

It is certainly reasonable that elected attorneys general act as the peoples' representative to ensure reelection. It is also likely that they see accountability not only through reelection campaigns, but also through an eventual campaign for the office.

"[T]he Office of the Attorney General has long been seen by many of its occupants as a stepping stone to the Governor's office . . . ." Marshall, *supra* at 2453.

States as Laboratories of Democracy

"Laboratories of democracy" is a phrase popularized by U.S. Supreme Court Justice Louis Brandeis in *New State Ice Co. v. Liebmann* to describe how a "state may, if its citizens choose, serve as a laboratory;

and try novel social and economic experiments without risk to the rest of the country." 285 U.S. 262 (1932).

Many states have been laboratories for new ideas. For example, in 2012, Washington and Colorado passed laws legalizing marijuana use. Although marijuana use is illegal nationally and in most other states, Washington and Colorado are seeing whether drug legalization is a benefit or a detriment to society. If it goes well there, similar laws could pass in other states and eventually even the entire United States.

Political experiments like this have taken place throughout U.S. history. One more important example is a woman's right to vote. Though the nation as a whole did not permit women to vote until the passage of the 19th amendment in 1919, many states had given women the right to vote far earlier. Giving women the vote in Wyoming in 1869, Utah in 1870, Colorado in 1893, Washington State in 1910 and California in 1911 did not cause disaster. Since women successfully voted without any major calamity, other states gave women the right to vote, a trend that culminated in the passage of the 19th Amendment in 1920.

The laboratory state experiment with the election of attorneys general has largely been a success. That 43 states elect their attorneys general is evidence that the laboratory works. Of course, any system of elections is not flawless. We can elect incompetent and dishonest attorneys general.

However, the dispersion of political power between governing the state and prosecuting justice in the state has worked well. In general, concentration of political power is dangerous, while dispersing that power between two elected officials is a more cautious practice.

Lord Acton, (John Emerich Edward Dalberg Acton), an English historian, politician and writer, noted, "remember, where you have a concentration of power in a few hands, all too frequently men with the mentality of gangsters get control. History has proven that. All power corrupts; absolute power corrupts absolutely."

Loyalty

President Trump, and some other presidents including President Kennedy, expected his attorney general to be loyal to him personally. That is why President Trump fired his first attorney general, Jeff Sessions, and hired William Barr as a loyal guard dog.

Appointed state attorneys general likely feel increased loyalty to the governor and his or her party, and thus may face political pressure in this respect. Scott M. Matheson, Jr., *Constitutional Status and Role of the State Attorney General*, 6 U. Fla. J.L. & Pub. Policy 1, 3 (1993).

Therefore, an elected attorney general will likely be constrained by his ambition for higher office or re-election. In addition, state governments benefit from independent elections that establish a class of experienced executive officials who can be effectively evaluated and groomed for higher office.

Chapter Five

Kennedy's Attorney General

"All experience teaches that, whenever there is a great national establishment, employing large numbers of officials, the public must be reconciled to support many incompetent men; for such is the favoritism and nepotism. . ."

> *--Herman Melville, an American novelist,*
> *short story writer and poet of the*
> *American Renaissance period.*
> *Among his best-known work*
> *is his masterpiece, Moby-Dick*

"I can't see that it's wrong to give him a little legal experience before he goes out to practice law."

> *--John F. Kennedy*
> *on the appointment of his brother*
> *to be attorney general in a speech*
> *at the Gridiron Club in 1961.*

After winning the 1960 presidential election, President-elect John F. Kennedy appointed his younger brother attorney general. Robert Kennedy was 34 years old at the time and although he had distinguished himself in various capacities as a congressional staffer, he had never tried a case in court. *The New York Times* criticized President Kennedy for appoint his brother to be attorney general, "It is simply not good enough to name a bright young political manager...to a major post in the government."

The choice was controversial, with liberal publications including *The New York Times* and *The New Republic* calling him inexperienced and unqualified. Robert Kennedy had no experience in any state or federal court, causing the president to joke, with the quote at the beginning of this chapter.

However, Kennedy was hardly a novice as a lawyer, having gained significant experience conducting investigations and questioning witnesses as a Justice Department attorney and Senate committee counsel and staff director.

According to Bobby Baker, the Senate majority secretary and a protégé of Lyndon Johnson, President-elect Kennedy did not want to name his brother attorney general. However, their father, Joseph P. Kennedy, Jr., directed the president-elect to do so. As a favor to Vice President Lyndon Johnson, Baker persuaded the influential Southern senator Richard Russell to allow a voice vote to confirm the president's brother in January 1961. Lyndon Johnson told Kennedy that Bobby, "would have been lucky to get 40 votes" on a roll-call vote.

Robert Kennedy performed well in his confirmation hearing and chose what friend and biographer Arthur M. Schlesinger Jr. called an "outstand-ing" group of deputy and assistant attorneys general, including future Supreme Court Justice Byron White and Nicholas Katzenbach.

Bobby Kennedy's tenure as attorney general was the high-water mark of greatest power for the office — no previous United States attorney general had enjoyed such clear influence on all areas of policy during an administration. To a great extent President Kennedy sought the advice and counsel of his younger brother, with Robert being the president's closest political adviser. He was relied upon as both the president's primary source of administrative information, and as a general counsel with whom trust was implicit. He exercised widespread authority over every cabinet department, leading the Associated Press to dub him "Bobby—Washington's No. 2-man."

The president once remarked about his brother, "If I want something done and done immediately I rely on the Attorney General. He is very much the doer in this administration, and has an organizational gift I have rarely if ever seen surpassed."

Whether Robert F. Kennedy was a good attorney general or not is not the issue. The issue presented by this book is that the attorney general should be independent of the president of the United States. Clearly, Robert F. Kennedy was not independent of his brother—his father made sure of that.

Law Against Nepotism

After Robert Kennedy left the Justice Department his term of service inspired another accomplishment. His tenure had inspired Congress to prohibit nepotism in the appointment of all federal officials. In 1967 a new law was passed restricting any federal official from appointing or even advocating for the hiring of a relative if the official has any degree of jurisdiction over the proposed official's position.

This section of the Code has come to be known as the Bobby Kennedy Law. 5 U.S. Code § 3110. **Employment of relatives; restrictions.** The law provides:

> A public official (including the President) may not appoint, employ, promote, advance, or advocate for appointment, employment, promotion, or advancement, in or to a civilian position in the agency in which he is serving or over which he exercises jurisdiction or control any individual who is a relative of the public official.

The term "relative" was defined to include a sister, brother, son, daughter, son-in-law, daughter-in-law and other relatives. This law has been clearly violated by President Trump's appointment of his daughter Ivanka and son-in-law Jared Kushner to be his advisors. There is no exception in the law for those who are not paid.

I would be remiss if I did not mention some of Robert Kennedy's notable achievements which are detailed below.

Berlin

As one of the president's closest White House advisers, Bobby Kennedy played a crucial role in the events surrounding the Berlin Crisis of 1961. Operating mainly through a private back-channel connection to Soviet spy Georgi Bolshakov, he relayed important diplomatic communications between the American and Soviet governments. Most significantly, this con-nection helped the U.S. set up the Vienna Summit in June, 1961, and later to defuse the tank standoff in October, 1961 with the Soviets at Checkpoint Charlie, the dividing line between the U.S. and Soviet zones.

Organized Crime

As attorney general, Robert Kennedy pursued a relentless crusade against organized crime and the Mafia, sometimes disagreeing on strategy with FBI Director J. Edgar Hoover. According to Justice Department statistics, convictions against organized crime figures rose by 800 percent during his term. Kennedy worked to shift Hoover's focus away from communism, which Hoover saw as a more serious threat, to organized crime. According to James Neff, Kennedy's success in this endeavor was due to his brother's position, giving the attorney general leverage over Hoover. Biographer Richard Hack concluded that Hoover's dislike for Kennedy came from his being unable to control him.

Bobby Kennedy was relentless in his pursuit of Teamsters Union president Jimmy Hoffa, due to Hoffa's known corruption in financial and electoral matters, both personally and organizationally. The hatred between the two men was intense, with accusations of a personal vendetta – what Hoffa called a "blood feud" – exchanged between them. On July 7, 1961, after Hoffa was reelected to the Teamsters presidency, RFK told reporters the government's case against Hoffa had not been changed by what he called "a small group of teamsters" supporting him. In 1964 Hoffa was imprisoned for jury tampering. After learning of Hoffa's conviction by telephone, Kennedy issued congratulatory messages to the three prosecutors.

Civil Rights

Robert F. Kennedy expressed the administration's commitment to civil rights during a 1961 speech at the University of Georgia Law School: "We will not stand by or be aloof—we will move. I happen to believe that the 1954 decision was right. But my belief does not matter. It is now the law. Some of you may believe the decision was wrong. That does not matter. It is the law."

FBI Director J. Edgar Hoover viewed civil rights leader Martin Luther King Jr. as an upstart troublemaker, calling him an "enemy of the state." In February, 1962, Hoover presented Kennedy with allegations that some of King's close confidants and advisers were communists. Concerned about the allegations, the FBI deployed agents to monitor King in the following months. Kennedy warned King to discontinue the suspected associations.

In response, King agreed to ask suspected Communist Jack O'Dell to resign from the SCLC, but refused to heed to the request to ask Stanley Levison, whom he regarded as a trusted advisor, to resign. In October 1963, Robert Kennedy issued a written directive authorizing the FBI to wiretap King and other leaders of the Southern Christian Leadership Conference, King's civil rights organization. Although Kennedy only gave written approval for limited wiretapping of King's phones "on a trial basis, for a month or so," Hoover extended the clearance so that his men were "unshackled" to look for evidence in any areas of King's life they deemed worthy. The wiretapping continued through June, 1966 and was revealed in 1968, days before Kennedy's assassination.

Robert Kennedy remained committed to civil rights enforcement to such a degree that he commented in 1962 that it seemed to envelop almost every area of his public and private life, from prosecuting corrupt Southern electoral officials to answering late night calls from Coretta Scott King concerning the imprisonment of her husband for demonstrations in Alabama. During his tenure as attorney general, he undertook the most energetic and persistent desegregation of the administration that Washington had ever experienced. He demanded that every area of government begin recruiting realistic levels of black and other ethnic workers, going so far as to criticize Vice President Johnson for his failure to desegregate his own office staff.

It has become commonplace to assert the phrase "The Kennedy Administration" or even "President Kennedy" when discussing the legislative and executive support of the civil rights movement. Between 1960 and 1963 a great many of the initiatives that occurred during Bobby Kennedy's tenure were the result of the passion and determination of an emboldened attorney general, who, through his rapid education in the realities of Southern racism, underwent a thorough conversion of purpose. .Asked in an interview in May, 1962, "What do you see as the big problem ahead for you, is it crime or internal security?" Kennedy replied, "Civil rights." The president came to share his brother's sense of urgency on the matters at hand to such an extent that it was at the attorney general's insistence that he made his famous June ,1963 address to the nation on civil rights.

Robert Kennedy played a large role in the response to the Freedom Riders protests. He acted after Anniston bus bombings to protect the Riders in continuing their journey, sending John Seigenthaler, his administrative assistant, to Alabama to attempt to secure the Riders' safety. Despite a work rule which allowed a driver to decline an assignment which he regarded as a potentially unsafe one, he persuaded a manager of The Greyhound Corporation to obtain a coach operator who was willing to drive a special bus for the continuance of the Freedom Ride from Birmingham, Alabama, to Montgomery, Alabama, on the circuitous journey to Jackson, Mississippi.

During the attack and burning by a white mob of the First Baptist Church in Montgomery, Alabama at which Martin Luther King Jr. and some 1,500 sympathizers were in attendance, the attorney general telephoned King to ask for his assurance that they would not leave the building until the force of U.S. Marshals and National Guard he sent had secured the area. King proceeded to berate Kennedy for "allowing the situation to continue." King later publicly thanked him for dispatching the forces to break up the attack that might otherwise have endangered his life. Kennedy then negotiated the safe passage of the Freedom Riders from the First Baptist Church to Jackson, Mississippi, where they were arrested. He offered to bail the Freedom Riders out of jail, but they refused, which upset him.

In September 1962, Robert Kennedy sent U.S. marshals to Oxford, Mississippi, to enforce a federal court order allowing the admittance of the first African-American student, James Meredith, to the University of Mississippi. The attorney general had hoped that legal means, along with the escort of U.S. marshals, would be enough to force Governor Ross Barnett to allow Meredith's admission. He also was very concerned there might be a "mini-civil war" between U.S. Army troops and armed protesters. President Kennedy reluctantly sent federal troops after the situation on campus turned violent.

Ensuing riots during the period of Meredith's admittance resulted in hundreds of injuries and two deaths, yet Robert Kennedy remained adamant that black students had the right to enjoy the benefits of all levels of the educational system. The Office of Civil Rights also hired its first African-American lawyer and began to work cautiously with leaders of the Civil Rights Movement. Bobby Kennedy saw voting as the key to racial justice and collaborated with presidents Kennedy and Johnson to create the landmark Civil Rights Act of 1964, which helped bring an end to Jim

Crow laws. Between December 1961 and December 1963, Attorney General Kennedy expanded the United States Department of Justice Civil Rights Division by 60 percent.

Legacy

Bobby Kennedy's legacy is both positive and negative. He undeniably gave birth to the anti-nepotism law. His active role in protecting civil rights protestors in the South will certainly go down in history as crucial to the nation's movement toward racial justice.

Bobby was more political than an attorney general should be. He was the number two power in Washington, D.C. Obviously, he was too close to his brother John. An attorney general should not be appointed by the president, should not be the president's brother, cousin or uncle. The attorney general should be independent of the White House and view legal issues from a legal, not political perspective.

Chapter Six

Nixon's Attorneys General

"When told that the Washington Post would publish a story linking Mitchell to payments to the Watergate burglary, Mitchell proclaimed, All that crap, you're putting it in the paper? It's all been denied. Katie Graham's (Washington Post publisher) gonna get her tit caught in a big fat wringer if that's published. Good Christ! That's the most sickening thing I ever heard."

—John Mitchell to Carl Bernstein, September 28, 1972.

John Mitchell

John Mitchell was Nixon's first attorney general. Mitchell was a former Nixon law partner who resigned from the Justice Department to run the Committee to Re-Elect the President. He was imprisoned for 19 months for approving the Watergate break-in and payoffs to keep it quiet. He died in 1988 of a heart attached at the age of 75.

While at the Justice Department, Mitchell personally approved the illegal COINTELPRO surveillance of antiwar and civil rights activists. He left his post to manage Nixon's 1972 campaign, there performing the acts of presidential loyalty that led to his conviction for conspiracy, obstruction of justice, false statements and perjury in the Watergate trials.

In the days immediately after the Watergate break-in of June 17, 1972, Mitchell enlisted former FBI agent Steve King to prevent his wife Martha from learning about the break-in or contacting reporters. While she was on a phone call with United Press journalist Helen Thomas about the break-in, King pulled the phone cord from the wall. Mrs. Mitchell was held against her will in a California hotel room and forcefully sedated by a psychiatrist after a physical struggle with five men that left her needing stitches.

Nixon aides, in an effort to discredit her, told the press that she had a "drinking problem." Nixon was later to tell interviewer David Frost in 1977 that Martha was a distraction to John Mitchell, such that no one was minding the store, and "If it hadn't been for Martha Mitchell, there'd have been no Watergate."

In 1972, when asked to comment about a forthcoming article that reported that Mitchell controlled a political slush fund used for gathering intelligence on the Democrats, he famously uttered an implied threat to reporter Carl Bernstein: "Katie Graham's gonna get her tit caught in a big fat wringer if that's published."

On February 21, 1975, Mitchell, who was represented by the criminal defense attorney William G. Hundley, was found guilty of conspiracy, obstruction of justice, and perjury and sentenced to two and a half to eight years in prison for his role in the Watergate break-in and cover-up, which he dubbed the "White House horrors." As a result of the conviction, Mitchell was disbarred from the practice of law in New York. The sentence was later reduced to one to four years by United States district court Judge John J. Sirica. Mitchell served only 19 months of his sentence at Federal Prison Camp, Montgomery (in Maxwell Air Force Base) in Montgomery, Alabama, a minimum-security prison, before being released on parole for medical reasons.

Tape recordings made by President Nixon and the testimony of others involved confirmed that Mitchell had participated in meetings to plan the break-in of the Democratic Party's national headquarters in the Watergate Hotel. In addition, he had met with the president on at least three occasions in an effort to cover up White House involvement after the burglars were discovered and arrested.

John Mitchell was never tried for having his wife kidnapped.

Elliott Richardson

Richardson was appointed United States Secretary of Defense on January 30, 1973. Richardson would serve as Secretary of Defense for four months before becoming Nixon's Attorney General, a move that would put him in the middle of the Watergate swamp.

In October, 1973, after Richardson had served five months as Attorney General, President Nixon ordered him to fire the top lawyer investigating the Watergate scandal, Special Prosecutor Archibald Cox.

Saturday Night Massacre

The Saturday Night Massacre refers to a series of events that took place in Washington, D.C. on the evening of Saturday, October 20, 1973. When Richard Nixon ordered Elliot Richardson to fire Special Prosecutor Archibald Cox, Richardson refused and resigned effective immediately. Nixon then ordered Deputy Attorney General William Ruckelshaus to fire Cox. Ruckelshaus refused, and also resigned. Nixon then ordered the third-most-senior official at the Justice Department, Solicitor General Robert Bork, to fire Cox. Bork carried out the order as Nixon asked. Bork claimed that he intended to resign afterward, but was persuaded by Richardson and Ruckelshaus to stay on for the good of the Justice Department.

The political and public reactions to Nixon's actions were exceptionally negative and highly damaging to the president.

The impeachment process against Richard Nixon began 10 days later, on October 30, 1973. Two days later Leon Jaworski was appointed as the new special prosecutor.

Richardson had appointed Cox in May, 1973 after promising the House Judiciary Committee that he would appoint a special prosecutor to investigate the events surrounding the break-in of the Democratic National Committee's offices at the Watergate Hotel in Washington, D.C., on June 17, 1972. The appointment was created as a career reserved position in the Justice department, meaning it came under the authority of the attorney general who could only remove the special prosecutor "for cause, such as gross improprieties or malfeasance in office. Richardson had, in his confirmation hearings before the U.S. Senate, promised not to use his authority to dismiss the Watergate special prosecutor, unless for good cause.

When Cox issued a subpoena to Nixon, asking for copies of taped conversations recorded in the Oval Office, the president refused to comply. On Friday, October 19, 1973, Nixon offered what was later known as the Stennis Compromise—asking the infamously hard-of-hearing Senator John C. Stennis of Mississippi to review and summarize the tapes for the special prosecutor's office. Cox refused the compromise that same evening, and it was believed that there would be a short rest in the legal maneuvering while government offices were closed for the weekend.

However, on the following day (Saturday), Nixon ordered Attorney General Richardson to fire Cox. Both Richardson and Ruckelshaus had given personal assurances to Congressional oversight committees that they would not interfere, but Bork had not. Although Bork later claimed he believed Nixon's order to be valid and appropriate, he still considered resigning to avoid being "perceived as a man who did the President's bidding to save my job." Nevertheless, having been brought to the White House by limousine and sworn in as acting attorney general, Bork wrote the letter dismissing Cox.

Robert Bork and William Saxbe

Robert Bork became so infamous that his name became a verb. "To Bork" someone means "to obstruct (someone, especially a candidate for public office) through systematic defamation or vilification."

Bork remained acting attorney general for less than three months until the appointment of Senator William B. Saxbe (R. Ohio) on January 4, 1974. Nixon resigned on August 8, 1974 after Senator Barry Goldwater and other Republicans informed the president that he would not survive impeachment.

In his posthumously published memoirs, Bork claimed that after he carried out the order, Nixon promised him the next seat on the Supreme Court, though Bork didn't take the offer seriously as he believed that Watergate had left Nixon too politically compromised to appoint another justice. Nixon would never get the chance to carry out his promise to Bork, as the next Supreme Court vacancy came after Nixon resigned and Gerald Ford assumed the presidency, with Ford instead nominating John Paul Stevens following the 1975 retirement of William O. Douglas.

On July 31, 1987, President Ronald Reagan nominated Judge Robert Bork for Associate Justice of the Supreme Court of the United

States to succeed Lewis Powell, who had earlier announced his retirement. On October 23, 1987, the Senate rejected Robert Bork's nomination to the Supreme Court by a Roll call vote of 42–58. Bork was borked. Note: I was one of many witnesses who testified against Robert Bork's confirmation. I stated that Bork fit the profile of the justices who had written the worst decisions of the Supreme Court, as noted in my book *Black Mondays: Worst Decision of the Supreme Court.*

Conclusion

President Nixon's dealing with his attorneys general is one of the best arguments for creating the office of an independent and elected attorney general. Nixon improperly terminated AG Elliot Richardson for not firing the Special Prosecutor. Special prosecutors would not be necessary if attorneys general were truly independent.

Chapter Seven

Ronald Reagan's Attorneys General

"But the thing is, you don't have many suspects who are innocent of a crime. That's contradictory. If a person is innocent of a crime, then he is not a suspect."

-- Ed Meese

William French Smith

William French Smith met Mr. Reagan before the 1966 campaign for governor of California, eventually becoming a member of the influential circle of advisers who formed the new Governor's "kitchen cabinet." Smith served as Ronald Reagan's personal lawyer in California and then accompanied him to Washington as his first Attorney General.

On December 11, 1980, Smith was nominated as the 74th Attorney General by the newly elected President Reagan. He assumed his position at the Department of Justice, on January 23, 1981, serving until February 25, 1985. Smith pursued a strong anti-crime initiative, increasing the resources used to fight the distribution and sale of illegal narcotics by 100 percent. He successfully lobbied for the establishment of a commission to create new federal sentencing guidelines.

William Smith's contributions were recommending a comprehensive crime package of more than 150 administrative and legislative initiatives (which included a federal death penalty), the denial of bail for certain types of crimes, the modification of the rule barring the use of illegally seized evidence in criminal trials, mandatory prison sentences for crimes involving the use of guns, and the use of private Internal Revenue Service information in combating organized crime. He also designed an immigration and refugee policy, announced a more lenient attitude towards corporate mergers in order to make government more responsive to the concerns of business, opposed anti competitive practices, and modified the Freedom of Information Act of 1966, among many other initiatives. Notable among these are the bills which passed in 1984 relating to immigration and crime.

President Ronald Reagan said this about Smith during a speech announcing the Federal Initiatives Against Drug Trafficking and Organized Crime:

> A few months ago Attorney General William French Smith and his staff, in collaboration with the Treasury Depart-

ment, put together final plans for a national strategy to expose, prosecute, and ultimately cripple organized crime in America. And I want to announce this program today. It is one that outlines a national strategy that I believe will bring us very close to removing a stain from American history that has lasted nearly a hundred years.

The American people want the mob and its associates brought to justice and their power broken—not out of a sense of vengeance, but out of a sense of justice; not just from an obligation to punish the guilty but from an even stronger obligation to protect the innocent; not simply for the sake of legalities but for the sake of the law that is the protection of liberty.

Attorney General Smith also was credited with playing a major role in Mr. Reagan's nomination of Sandra Day O'Connor to be the first woman on the Supreme Court. His term as Attorney General was fairly uncontroversial compared to his successor.

Ed Meese

Following the Iowa caucuses, Ed Meese joined the 1980 Reagan presidential campaign full-time as chief of staff in charge of day-to-day campaign operations and senior issues adviser. After the 1980 election, Meese headed Reagan's transition effort.

On the advice of Meese, Reagan secretly allowed his campaign to establish a transition office to avoid difficulties similar to those faced by the Nixon administration in its own transition. "Ed had an uncanny ability to look down the road," said Pen James, Assistant to the President for Presidential Personnel. Meese's presidential transition team employed more than 1,000 individuals.

Meese became Counselor to the President, who appointed him as a member of both his Cabinet and the National Security Council from 1981 to 1985. On Monday, September 14, 1981, Meese chaired the first White House discussion of what would become Reagan's Strategic Defense Initiative (SDI), the missile defense system.

Reagan nominated Meese to be William French Smith's successor as Attorney General on January 23, 1984. For more than a year, Democrats repeatedly charged Meese with unethical conduct to bar his confirmation as attorney general, including a report by Archibald Cox to the Senate on Meese's "lack of ethical sensitivity" and "blindness to abuse of position." However, he was finally confirmed by a vote of 63–31, with more opposition than any other Attorney General nominee had received since the 1920s. Meese became Attorney General in February 1985

Iran-Contra Scandal

One of the most significant foreign policy scandals of the last half-century was the Iran-Contra affair, in which the Reagan Administration, prodded by CIA Director William Casey and NSC Advisor Oliver North, secretly arranged for an arms-for-hostage deal with Iran. Israel sold weapons from the U.S. to Iran, which had been designated a State Sponsor of Terrorism in 1984 and the subject of an arms embargo, in exchange for the release of American hostages held by Hezbollah, Iran's ally, in Lebanon.

Oliver North and William Casey funneling the profits from the arms sales into yet another illegal venture, a secret plan to support the Contras, the militants in Nicaragua, who opposed the communist Sandinistas. This was in direct contravention of the Boland Amendment, which Congress had passed from 1982-84, specifically prohibiting U.S. support of the Contras.

The entire plot unraveled on November 3, 1986, when the Beirut newspaper *Al Shiraa*, revealed the arms-for-hostages deal. North destroyed or hid pertinent documents between November 21- 25, 1986.

Attorney General Edwin Meese admitted on November 25 that profits from the weapons sales were aiding the Contras. On the same day, National Security Advisor John Poindexter resigned, and Oliver North was fired by President Reagan.

Congressional investigations were initiated and widespread criticism and outrage over the scheme forced Reagan to apologize on a nationally televised address on March 4, 1987.

Several high-ranking Administration officials were indicted on various charges related to Iran-Contra including Secretary of Defense Caspar Weinberger on two counts of perjury and one count of obstruction of justice on June 16, 1992. Weinberger received a pardon from President George H.W. Bush in December 1992, before he was tried. William Casey, who was the mastermind of the plot, fell ill hours before he would testify.

National Security Adviser Robert C. McFarlane was convicted of withholding evidence, but after a plea bargain was given only two years of probation. McFarlane was also pardoned by President George H. W. Bush.

Elliott Abrams, then Assistant Secretary of State, was convicted of withholding evidence, but after a plea bargain was given only two-years probation. He was also pardoned by President Bush. Clair George, Chief of Covert Ops at the CIA, was convicted on two charges of perjury, but was also pardoned by President Bush before sentencing.

Oliver North, member of the National Security Council, was convicted of accepting an illegal gratuity, obstruction of a Congressional inquiry, and destruction of documents, but the ruling was overturned since he had been granted immunity.

Meese was investigated for his role in covering up the Iran-Contra Affair to limit damage to President Ronald Reagan. Although evidence supporting this accusation came to light, Meese was ultimately not charged with any obstruction of justice or any other crimes.

The Wedtech Scandal

In February, 1987, James C. McKay was named independent counsel in the Wedtech case. The investigation centered on actions Meese took that benefited him and his longtime friend and former lawyer, E. Robert Wallach. McKay looked into Meese's involvement while Attorney General, in negotiations involving the company Wedtech. E. Robert Wallach worked as a lobbyist for the company and sought help from Meese on Wedtech contract matters.

McKay never prosecuted nor sought indictment of Meese, but in his official report, which is still confidential, he was highly critical of Meese's ethics and urged further investigation of Meese's role in that scandal and others such as Meese's efforts to help Bechtel Corporation. Meese falsely claimed the report was a "full vindication." While Meese was never convicted of any wrongdoing, he resigned in 1988 when the independent counsel delivered the report. Prior to his resignation, several top Justice Department officials resigned in protest of what they and others viewed as improper acts by the Attorney General.

Reagan publicly voiced support for Meese in his role as Attorney General during a press conference: "If Ed Meese is not a good man, there are no good men."

Meese Report on Pornography

On May 21, 1984, Reagan announced his intention to appoint the Attorney General to study the effect of pornography on society. The Attorney General Commission on Pornography produced the Meese Report published in July, 1986. The Meese Report advised that pornography was harmful. Following the release of the report, guidelines of the Meese-led Department of Justice were modified to enable the government to file multiple cases in various jurisdictions at the same time which eroded some of the markets for pornography.

Drug Control Policy

As Attorney General, Ed Meese chaired the National Drug Policy Board, which coordinated with Nancy Reagan's "Just Say No," national anti-drug educational campaign. One of Meese's innovations was to seek the cooperation of drug-producing countries.

"One of our most effective weapons against drug traffickers," Meese wrote in his autobiography, "was to confiscate the assets of their criminal activity, such as expensive autos, yachts, businesses and homes.... To make this technique even more effective, we shared the proceeds with cooperating local law enforcement agencies to enhance their drug-fighting activities."

Conclusion

Both of President Reagan's attorney's general were close friends of the president and would do everything within their power to protect him. William French Smith was Reagan's personal attorney before becoming Attorney General and he stayed, in effect, Reagan's personal attorney.

Ed Meese was counsel to Reagan in the White House and a key political operative during the campaign. He successfully kept himself and Reagan out of trouble concerning the Iran-Contra Affair.

Neither Smith nor Meese were independent attorneys general. Attorneys General should be legal counsel, not political counsel. They should represent the interests of the United States, not the president.

The careers of both Smith and Meese make a strong case for replacing the appointment of attorneys general with the election of attorneys general.

Chapter Eight

George W. Bush's Attorneys General

"President Bush delivered his first state of the union address, riding high with an 82 percent approval rating, and with John Ashcroft dispatching agents interviewing the other 18 percent."

--Jon Stewart, The Daily Show, 2001

John Ashcroft

In December, 2000, following his Senatorial defeat, John Ashcroft was chosen for the position of U.S. attorney general by president-elect George W. Bush.

After the September 11, 2001 attacks in the United States, Ashcroft was a key administration supporter of passage of the USA Patriot Act. One of its provisions, Section 215, allows the Federal Bureau of

Investigation (FBI) to apply for an order from the Foreign Intelligence Surveillance Court to require production of "any tangible thing" for an investigation. This provision was criticized by citizen and professional groups concerned about violations of privacy. Ashcroft referred to the American Library Association's opposition to Section 215 as "hysteria" in two separate speeches given in September, 2003.

In 2002, under Ashcroft, curtains were installed blocking the Spirit of Justice statue in the Robert F. Kennedy Department of Justice Building, which is of a woman wearing a toga-like dress with one breast revealed, from view during speeches.

In March, 2004, the Justice Department under Ashcroft ruled that the President Bush's domestic intelligence program—code name Stellar Wind was illegal. After the ruling, Ashcroft became critically ill with acute pancreatitis. President Bush's White House Counsel, Alberto Gonzales, and his Chief of Staff, Andrew Card Jr., went to Ashcroft's bedside in the hospital intensive-care unit, to persuade the incapacitated Attorney General to sign a document to "reauthorize" the program that Justice had declared illegal and at end. According to his account before the Senate Judiciary Committee, Acting Attorney General James

Comey alerted then-FBI Director Robert Mueller III of the reauthorization plan, and "raced" to the hospital, sirens blaring, arriving ahead of Gonzales and Card, Jr. Ashcroft, "summoning the strength to lift his head and speak, refused to sign. Jack Goldsmith, head of the Office of Legal Counsel for Justice, was also there to support Ashcroft was Patrick Philbin, an Associate Deputy Attorney General (according to congressional testimony from Comey).   FBI Director Robert Mueller, who also was rushing to George Washington University hospital, spoke by phone to Ashcroft's security detail, ordering them not to allow Card or Gonzales to have Comey removed from the hospital room.

In 2008, we learned that another issue of contention wasn't warrantless wiretapping, but rather another form of data mining. The controversy specifically involved Internet, not telephone, metadata. STELLAR WIND had four components, each corresponding to types of information that President Bush had authorized the NSA to collect without a court order:

- telephone content (i.e., warrantless wiretapping)
- Internet content
- telephone metadata (i.e., the massive call records database)
- Internet metadata

The administration had originally carried out this surveillance on a radical theory of "inherent presidential authority" spelled out by then–Justice Department lawyer John Yoo, which held that during wartime, the president's surveillance powers could not be constrained by Congress, or even the Fourth Amendment. After he returned to academia in 2003, however, his successors grew uncomfortable with his leaps of legal logic and stopped relying on his questionable opinions on a broad range of counterterrorism issues. To justify Bush's surveillance programs, DOJ lawyers switched to the theory, spelled out at length in a January, 2006 memorandum that Congress's Authorization for the Use of Military Force (AUMF) against Al Qaeda and their affiliates had created a tacit exception to the Foreign Intelligence Surveillance Act (FISA).

Though FISA is supposed to be the "exclusive means" by which intelligence surveillance is conducted, DOJ attorneys argued that the AUMF authority to use "all necessary and appropriate force" against those who the president "determines planned, authorized, committed or aided" the September 11 attacks necessarily included the power to conduct surveillance, superseding FISA's judicial review requirements.

That was quite a different argument than Yoo's argument, though still a problematic twist of legal reasoning: Congress, after all, explicitly expanded the government's surveillance powers in the USA Patriot Act.

Ashcroft was released from the hospital on March 14, 2004 and remained attorney general until November 9, 2004. Ashcroft announced his resignation, which took effect on February 3, 2005, after the Senate confirmed White House Counsel Alberto Gonzales as the next attorney general.

Alberto Gonzales

Appointed in February, 2005 by President George W. Bush, at the start of his second term, becoming the highest-ranking Hispanic American in executive government to date. When Gonzales fired eight United States attorneys because they were not aggressive enough in prosecuting Democrats, the outrage was bipartisan, and he was forced to resign.

He was also the first Hispanic to serve as White House Counsel. Earlier he had been Bush's General Counsel during his governorship of Texas. Gonzales had also served as Secretary of State of Texas and then as a Texas Supreme Court Justice.

Gonzales's tenure as U.S. Attorney General was marked by controversy regarding warrantless surveillance of U.S. citizens and the legal authorization of so-called "enhanced interrogation techniques," a euphemism for torture, in the U.S. government's post-9/11 "War on Terror." Gonzales had also presided over the firings of several U.S. Attorneys who had refused back-channel White House directives to prosecute political enemies, allegedly causing the office of Attorney General to become improperly politicized. Following calls for his removal, Gonzales resigned from the office "in the best interests of the department," on August 27, 2007, effective September 17, 2007.

A number of members of both houses of Congress publicly said Gonzales should resign or be fired by President Bush. Calls for his ousting intensified after his testimony on April 19, 2007. However, the President gave Gonzales a strong vote of confidence saying, "This is an honest, honorable man, in whom I have confidence." The President said that Gonzales's testimony "increased my confidence" in his ability to lead the Justice Department. Separately, a White House spokeswoman said, "He's staying."

On May 24, 2007, Senators Charles Schumer (D-NY), Dianne Feinstein (D-CA), and Sheldon Whitehouse (D-RI) of the Senate Judiciary Committee announced the Democrats' proposed no-confidence resolution to vote on whether "Attorney General Alberto Gonzales no longer holds the confidence of the Senate and the American People." (The vote would have had no legal effect, but was designed to persuade Gonzales to resign or President Bush to seek a new attorney general.) A similar resolution was introduced in the House by Rep. Adam Schiff (DCA).

On June 11, 2007 a Senate vote on cloture to end debate on the resolution failed (60 votes are required for cloture). The vote was 53 to 38 with 7 not voting and 1 voting "present" (one senate seat was vacant).

Seven Republicans, John E. Sununu, Chuck Hagel, Susan Collins, Arlen Specter, Olympia Snowe, Gordon Smith and Norm Coleman voted to end debate; Independent Democrat Joseph Lieberman voted against ending debate. No Democrat voted against the motion. Not voting: Joe Biden (D-DE), Brownback (R-KS), Coburn (R-OK), Dodd (D-CT), Johnson (D-SD), Mc-Cain (R-AZ), Obama (D-IL). Stevens (R-AK) voted "present."

On July 30, 2007, MSNBC reported that Rep. Jay Inslee announced that he would introduce a bill the following day that would require the House Judiciary Committee to begin an impeachment investigation against Gonzales.

Michael Mukasey

On September 17, 2007, Mukasey was nominated by President Bush to replace Alberto Gonzales as the Attorney General. During confirmation hearings, controversy arose over Mukasey's responses to questions about torture. Mukasey refused to state a clear legal position on the interrogation technique known as waterboarding (in which water is poured over a rag on the prisoner's face to simulate drowning). Senator Leahy and the other nine Democratic committee members indicated to Mukasey, via letter, that they were "deeply troubled by your refusal to state unequivocally that waterboarding is illegal during your confirmation hearing." Five senators–Christopher Dodd of Connecticut, Joseph Biden of Delaware, John Kerry of Massachusetts, Edward Kennedy of Massachusetts and Bernie Sanders of Vermont – in addition to Leahy had announced their intention to vote against Mukasey's confirmation due to concerns about his stance on torture.

Despite opposition to Mukasey's appointment, on November 6, 2007 the Senate Judiciary Committee approved his nomination , by an 11 to 8 vote, and sent his confirmation on to the full Senate. Two days later, the Senate confirmed Mukasey by a 53–40 vote. The close vote was the narrowest margin to confirm an attorney general in more than 50 years.

In a 2008 hearing, Mukasey said waterboarding would feel like torture if he were subjected to it. But Mukasey was still in favor of using "enhanced interrogation" techniques. Asked directly if Michael Mukasey was a liar because he claimed that enhanced interrogation produced useful intelligence, Sen. John McCain stated unequivocally, "Yes, I know that he is. Even if we had gotten useful information, the propaganda and the image and the behavior of the greatest nation on earth from torturing people is not what we want and it helps the enemy."

Conclusion

President Bush used his attorneys general to advance his political agenda. Attorney General Gonzales fired numerous U.S. attorneys because they did not pursue criminal prosecution of democrats. The attorney general should never use his office to punish the political opposition. This is the hallmark of a banana republic whose first inclination is to prosecute those who lost the last election. This is a compelling argument for creating an independent, separately elected, attorney general.

George W. Bush's attorneys general justified torture, wiretapping and mass surveillance of citizens. Not exactly the thoughtful attorneys like Robert F. Kennedy and Edmund Randolph. But Bush's attorneys general were his faithful political allies, always backing up his questionable policies. All three of these gems make the case for an independent-elected independent attorney general.

Chapter Nine

Obama's Attorneys General

"Under Attorney General Eric H. Holder Jr., the Justice Department prosecuted more people for having unauthorized discussions with reporters than all prior administrations combined."

—Matt Apuzzo,
New York Times Pulitzer-Prize-winning journalist

Eric Holder

Eric Himpton Holder Jr. (born January 21, 1951) is an American lawyer who served as the 82nd At-torney General of the United States from 2009 to 2015. Holder, serving in the administration of President Barack Obama, was the first African American to hold the position of U.S. Attorney General (in both a confirmed and acting position).

After graduating law school, Holder worked for the Public Integrity Section of the Department of Justice for 12 years. He next served as a judge of the Superior Court of the District of Columbia before being appointed by President Bill Clinton as United States Attorney for the District of Columbia and subsequently Deputy Attorney General. While U.S. Attorney, he prosecuted Democratic Congressman Dan Rostenkowski for corruption charges related to his role in the Congressional Post Office scandal.

Holder was senior legal advisor to Barack Obama during Obama's presidential campaign and one of three members of Obama's Vice-Presidential selection committee. Holder was and remains a close ally and confidant of Obama.

Contempt of Congress

Holder became the first sitting Attorney General to be held in contempt of Congress during an investigation of the Operation Fast and Furious ATF gunrunning scandal. The ATF, Alcohol, Tobacco and Firearms bureau, is a division of the Department of Justice.

"Fast and Furious" was an operation so secret that Mexican authorities weren't notified that thousands of semi-automatic firearms were being sold to arms dealers in Arizona thought to have links to Mexican drug cartels.

In 2009, According to ATF whistleblowers, the U.S. government began instructing gun storeowners to break the law by selling firearms to suspected criminals. ATF agents then, again according to testimony by ATF whistleblowers, were ordered not to intercept the smugglers but rather to let the guns "walk" across the U.S.-Mexican border and into the hands of Mexican drug-trafficking organizations.

In the fall of 2009, ATF agents began pressuring gun storeowners in Arizona to sell firearms to gunrunners the ATF thought would sell the guns to Mexican cartels and gangs. As gun-storeowners can't do business without federal licenses, and because the ATF has the authority to shut down a gun store if the store's paperwork isn't in order, these requests were taken as orders. This put the gun storeowners in a horrible situation: the law requires licensed gun stores to report suspicious activity and not to sell to people they think are breaking the law. But the ATF was telling them to sell to suspicious people who wanted to buy AK-47s by the dozen, several of whom were convicted felons.

ATF field agents began to question the sanity of letting guns "walk" across the border. ATF Special Agent Olindo James Casa testified before a Congressional Oversight Committee on June 15, 2011, "on several occasions I personally requested to interdict or seize firearms, but I was always ordered to stand down and not to seize the firearms."

As many ATF agents feared, on December 14, 2010, at night in a remote canyon in Rio Rico, Arizona, some of the firearms sent over the border to arm Mexican drug runners were used in a gun battle with the U.S. Border Patrol. During the gunfight, U.S. Border Patrol Agent Brian Terry, 40, was killed by suspected operatives of a Mexican drug-smuggling organization. After the battle that U.S. Border Patrol officers started by shooting bean bags at smugglers armed with AK-47s, police arrested four suspects and recovered three firearms that have since been traced to Fast and Furious.

On March 22, 2011, President Obama was asked about Operation Fast and Furious. The question came from a journalist from Univision, a Spanish-language network. President Obama said, "I did not authorize [Fast and Furious]. Eric Holder, the attorney general, did not authorize it. There may be a situation here in which a serious mistake was made. If that's the case, then we'll find--find out and we'll hold somebody accountable."

On May 3, 2011, Attorney General Holder testified before the House Judiciary Committee. Holder testified, "I probably heard about Fast and Furious for the first time over the last few weeks."

Two months later, on July 4, 2011, acting ATF Director Kenneth Melson was interviewed by congressional investigators from the House Oversight and Government Reform Committee and the Senate Judiciary Committee. Melson met with investigators with his personal attorney present—not Justice Department attorneys. The next day Senator Grassley (R. Iowa) wrote a letter to Attorney General Holder about Melson's testimony. The letter stated that Melson, "claimed that ATF's senior leadership would have preferred to be more cooperative with our inquiry much earlier in the process. However, he said that Justice Department officials directed them not to respond and took full control of replying to briefing and document requests from Congress." After his testimony, the U.S. Justice Department transferred Melson to a new post inside the ATF, a position that protected his retirement package.

During this undercover operation, federal agents tracked the sale of roughly 2,000 weapons to straw buyers working for Mexican drug cartels. The sting operation failed, and weapons related to the Fast and Furious program were found at the shooting scene when a Border Patrol agent was killed in December, 2010.

Relying on what they said was inaccurate information supplied by the Bureau of Alcohol, Tobacco, Firearms and Explosives - which comes under DOJ -

senior Justice officials told lawmakers in February, 2011 that no guns were allowed to "walk" to Mexico. That letter was later withdrawn by the Justice Department as inaccurate. Holder refused to turn over materials containing internal discussions, and asked President Obama to assert executive privilege over the documents. President Obama asserted executive privilege on only some of the documents Congress was seeking shortly before the Oversight and Government voted on party lines to approve a contempt resolution against Holder.

The Republican-controlled House of Representatives voted to hold Attorney General Eric Holder in contempt of Congress for his failure to turn over documents related to the Fast and Furious scandal, the first time Congress has taken such a dramatic move against a sitting Cabinet official.

The vote was 255-67, with 17 Democrats voting in support of a criminal contempt resolution, that authorized Republicans leaders to seek criminal charges against Eric Holder.

Defending U.S. Drone Strikes and Raids

As Attorney General, Holder was a staunch opponent of legal limitations on the executive branch's ability to prosecute the war on terror. In May, 2011,

Holder testified before Congress on the legality of the operation in which U.S. special forces killed Osama bin Laden earlier that month. Holder testified that the operation to kill bin Laden was legal, stating that international law allows for targeting enemy commanders. To support this point, Holder said that computer evidence seized from the raid demonstrated that bin Laden was still leading al-Qaeda. Moreover, Holder said, the Navy SEAL team that carried out the raid conducted itself in a manner consistent with American values, and that the parameters of the mission included capturing bin Laden.

Holder defended the legality of drone strikes against alleged terrorists. Addressing the death of Anwar al-Awlaki, an American citizen who was killed by drone strike without trial, Holder said, "The U.S. government's use of lethal force in self-defense against a leader of alQaeda or an associated force who presents an imminent threat of violent attack would not be unlawful." He outlined a three-part test to affirm the lawfulness of the strikes: the terrorist poses an imminent threat of violence to the United States, capture is not possible and the operation is conducted in a manner consistent with the principles of the law of war. At the time, al-Awlaki was an alleged leader and recruiter for Al-Qaeda in the Arabian Peninsula. Holder later stated that " '[d]ue process' and 'judicial process' are not one and the same, particularly when it comes to national security. The Constitution guarantees due process, not judicial process." Some civil liberties advocates have described the incident as "an extrajudicial execution" that breached al-Awlaki's right to due process, including a trial.

Terrorism Prosecutions

A major legacy of Holder's tenure as attorney general was a shifting of terrorism cases to the civilian federal courts. Under Holder, the DOJ successfully tried many terrorists in federal court, securing convictions and life sentences against a string of defendants, including Sulaiman Abu Ghaith (Osama bin Laden's spokesman); Ahmed Ghailani (a conspirator in the 1998 East Africa bombings); and Abu Hamza (an al-Qaeda operative). Faisal Shahzad (the attempted Times Square bomber); and Omar Farouk Abdulmutallab (the failed "underwear bomber") pleaded guilty in federal court and were sentenced to life imprisonment during Holder's term. During Holder's term, other terrorists—including Najibullah Zazi (who plotted a New York subway attack), and Ahmed Abdulkadir Warsame (an al-Shabab supporter) pleaded guilty and cooperated with the government.

Matt Olsen, the director of the National Counterterrorism Center from 2011 to 2014, wrote in 2015: "Through his persistence, Holder demonstrated the wisdom and value of prosecuting terrorists in civilian courts and cemented this approach for future administrations."

In November, 2009, Holder announced that September 11th attack co-conspirators—Khalid Sheikh Mohammed, Ramzi Bin alShibh, Walid bin Attash, Ali Abdul Aziz Ali and Mustafa Ahmed alHawsawi—would be tried in New York City on federal charges of conspiracy and murder. Holder said at the time that the five would "stand trial in our justice system before an impartial jury under long-established rules and procedures." This plan was frustrated by Congress, however, and congressional restrictions on transferring Guantánamo detainees to federal court delayed the cases indefinitely.

In April, 2011, Holder was forced to drop plans for a federal trial and instead refer the five to military commissions. Holder criticized Congress for interfering in the prosecution, saying: "[Congress has] taken one of the nation's most tested counterterrorism tools off the table and tied our hands in a way that would have serious ramifications."

Same-Sex Marriage

In February, 2011, Holder announced that the DOJ would no longer defend cases involving the Defense of Marriage Act in court. Holder had recommended this course of action to the President, arguing that the Defense of Marriage Act was unconstitutional, as laws that prohibit the marriage of gay couples do not meet the legal principle of strict scrutiny. Holder cited changing law in support of his action: "Much of the legal landscape has changed in the 15 years since Congress passed DOMA. The Supreme Court has ruled that laws criminalizing homosexual conduct are unconstitutional. Congress has repealed the military's 'Don't Ask, Don't Tell' policy. Several lower courts have ruled DOMA itself to be unconstitutional."

Leak Investigations

Under Holder's leadership, the Department of Justice brought six leak-related prosecutions against current or former U.S. government employees, while all previous administrations combined had tried a total of three such cases. Holder was reportedly surprised by news reports pointing out this statistic, and was said to have told associates that he did not wish to have leak prosecutions be his legacy. Several prominent leak prosecutions under Holder involved communications between criminal defendants and journalists, and the pervasive use of traceable electronic communications between journalists and their sources provided the prosecution with a tool to determine the potential origin of published information. Under Holder, the Justice Department argued that journalists had no legal protection to maintain the confidentiality of their sources, and can be compelled by the government to reveal them, or potentially face criminal contempt charges. On September 17, 2018, the Freedom of the Press Foundation obtained documents regarding the use of FISA courts to spy on journalists.

On May 13, 2013, the Associated Press reported that the telephone records for 20 of their reporters during a two-month period in 2012 had been seized by the Justice Department as part of the 2013 Department of

Justice investigations of reporters. The AP described these acts as a "massive and unprecedented intrusion" into their news-gathering operation.

Holder testified under oath before the House Judiciary Committee that he had recused himself from these leak investigations to avoid any appearance of a conflict of interest. Holder said his Deputy Attorney General, James Cole was in charge of the AP investigation and would've ordered the subpoenas. When questioning turned to the possibility of journalists being charged under the Espionage Act for reporting classified material, Holder stated: "With regard to the potential prosecution of the press for the disclosure of material, that is not something that I've ever been involved in, heard of or would think would be a wise policy."

It was later reported that the DOJ monitored James Rosen, a Fox News reporter, by tracking his visits to the State Department through phone traces, timing of calls and his personal emails. NBC confirmed with the Justice Department that Holder had personally signed off on the Rosen subpoenas. The DOJ defended their decision and spoke about a balance between protecting national secrets and the 1st Amendment, stating: "After extensive deliberations, and after following all applicable laws, regulations and policies, the Department sought an appropriately tailored search warrant under the Privacy Protection Act." The revelation brought into question whether Holder had been intentionally mis-leading during his previous testimony. House Committee members sent an open letter to Holder, saying: "It is imperative that the committee, the Con-gress, and the American people be provided a full and ac-curate account of your involvement."

Too Big to Fail

On March 6, 2013, Holder testified before the Senate Judiciary Committee that the size of large financial institutions has made it difficult for the Justice Department to bring criminal charges. When they are suspected of crimes, criminal charges can threaten the survival of a bank and therefore their interconnectedness may endanger the national or global economy. "Some of these institutions have become too large," Holder told the Committee, "It has an inhibiting impact on our ability to bring resolutions that I think would be more appropriate."

In a January 29, 2013 letter to Holder, Senators Sherrod Brown and Charles Grassley criticized this Justice Department policy citing "important questions about the Justice Department's prosecutorial philosophy." After receipt of a DOJ response letter, Brown and Grassley issued a statement saying, "The Justice Department's response is aggressively evasive. It does not answer our questions. We want to know how and why the Justice Department has determined that certain financial institutions are 'too big to jail' and that prosecuting those institutions would damage the financial system."

Resignation

Holder announced his resignation on September 25, 2014, citing personal reasons. He remained in office until the Senate confirmed his successor, Loretta Lynch.

Loretta Lynch

Loretta Lynch was confirmed by the Senate Judiciary Committee on February 26, 2015, and approved by the Senate in a 56-43 vote on April 23, thereby becoming the first African-American woman and the second African-American after Holder. She was also and the second woman AG after Janet Reno to hold this office.

Several Republicans on the Senate Judiciary Committee, including chairman Chuck Grassley, op-posed Lynch's confirmation, saying it was important to find out more about Lynch's role in settling a $1.9 billion money-laundering deal with HSBC when she served as United States Attorney in New York. Senator Rand Paul (R. Kentucky) opposed her nomination for her support of civil forfeiture. On April 23, 2015, cloture was invoked on her nomination by a vote of 66 to 34. Her appointment was confirmed the same day by a 56 to 43 vote. Lynch's nomination process was one of the longest in the history of the United States, taking 166 days after she was first nominated for the post

The Clinton Controversy

On June 27, 2016, Lynch and former President Bill Clinton met privately aboard Lynch's Justice Department jet, which was parked on the tarmac in Phoenix, Arizona. ABC15 Phoenix reporter Christopher Sign broke the story on June 29th. The following day, during a press conference in Phoenix, Lynch denied the conversation was about the Hillary Clinton email controversy or any matters pertaining to it, saying the discussion instead involved personal social topics such as travels, golf, and grandchildren.

On July 1, 2016, Lynch swore she would "fully accept" the recommendation of the FBI and prosecutors regarding the email probe, and admitted that she understood how the meeting was raising "questions and concerns," and that she "certainly wouldn't do it again."

FBI Director James Comey recommended not pressing charges against Hillary Clinton on July 16, 2016. On the same day, Lynch confirmed that the Justice Department had opted to not pursue charges against Clinton and would close the probe into her private email server.

On June 8, 2017, former FBI head James Comey testified under oath that Lynch had instructed him (during the course of a private conversation) to not refer to the Clinton email scandal as an "investigation" and instead refer to it as a "matter." He also said that the directive, combined with Lynch's Phoenix airport meeting with former President Clinton, led him to make his independent announcement regarding the Clinton email probe a year earlier. In his Senate Intelligence Committee testimony Comey said that tarmac meeting was a "deciding factor" in his decision to act alone to update the public on the Clinton probe— and protect the Bureau's reputation.

On June 2017, the Senate Judiciary Committee launched a bipartisan investigation into whether or not Lynch tried to interfere with the Hillary Clinton email investigation. The following month, Lynch issued a statement through her lawyer pledging to cooperate with the investigation and denying the allegation she had given assurances to a Clinton campaign staffer that she would limit the email investigation.

The Department of Justice Inspector General also investigated the handling of the Clinton email investigation. The Inspector General's report, released in June, 2018, called Lynch's tarmac meeting with Bill Clinton an error of judgment for the public perception it created, but found no political bias.

Conclusions

Both of Obama's attorneys general showed themselves to be political operatives, not independent judicial officials. AG Holder was a close friend of Obama's and served to protect Obama's political interests. He stonewalled the Fast and Furious investigation and became the only attorney general in history to be found in contempt of Congress.

Loretta Lynch never should have met with former President Clinton while the Justice Department and the FBI were investigating his wife Hilary Clinton. Hopefully, a truly independent attorney general would have told Bill Clinton to get off the plane and would not have met with him. In order to get politics out of the Justice Department we need to have an independently elected attorney general who does not serve at the pleasure of the President of the United States.

Chapter Ten

Trump's Attorneys Generals

"He puts the word 'justice' in quotes when he refers to the Department of Justice because he believes it is corrupt."

—Donald Trump on Fox & Friends, August, 2018

Jeff Sessions

In early November, 2017, Trump told reporters, "a lot of people are disappointed in the Justice Department, including me." He said he was "frustrated" that he could not direct the DOJ or the FBI to take action in specific cases, remarks that Justice Department veterans consider a serious breach of the wall between the department and the president. While the Department of Justice considers itself to be "independent" of the president, it is not. Jeff Sessions did try to keep his independence but President Trump would not stand for it—Trump wanted a yes man to head the Justice Department.

President Trump said that he never would have appointed Attorney General Jeff Sessions had he known Mr. Sessions would recuse himself from overseeing the Russia investigation that has dogged his presidency, calling the decision "very unfair to the president."

In a remarkable public break with one of his earliest political supporters, Mr. Trump complained that Mr. Sessions's decision ultimately led to the appointment of a special counsel that should not have happened. "Sessions should have never recused himself, and if he was going to recuse himself, he should have told me before he took the job and I would have picked somebody else," Mr. Trump said.

In a wide-ranging interview with *The New York Times,* the president also accused James B. Comey, the F.B.I. director that he fired in May, of trying to leverage a dossier of compromising material to keep his job. Mr. Trump criticized both the acting F.B.I. director who has been filling in since Mr. Comey's dismissal and the deputy attorney general who recommended it. And he took on Robert S. Mueller III, the special counsel now leading the investigation into Russian meddling in last year's election.

Mr. Trump said Mr. Mueller was running an office rife with conflicts of interest and warned investigators against delving into matters too far afield from Russia. Mr. Trump never said he would order the Justice

Department to fire Mr. Mueller, nor would he outline circumstances under which he might do so. But he left open the possibility as he expressed deep grievance over an investigation that has taken a political toll in the six months since he took office.

Sessions went out of his way to deny meeting with Russians during the 2016 presidential campaign. His former colleagues in the Senate approved the nomination 52 to 47, despite concerns about al-legations of racial insensitivity and hostility to civil rights in his past.

But Sessions soon ran into trouble. He was forced to correct his Senate testimony to indicate that he had, in fact, met with the Russian ambassador at least twice in 2016. Democrats on Capitol Hill accused him of making false statements. The disclosure provoked intense public scrutiny of his actions.

By March 2017, Sessions fielded questions almost daily about whether he could oversee the ongoing Department of Justice investigation into Russian interference in the election, given his vocal role in the campaign, in which he even donned a "Make America Great Again" hat to support Donald Trump.

Ultimately, after consulting with DOJ ethics officials, Sessions recused himself from the Russia probe. He cited long-standing rules regarding conflicts that arise when authorities investigate campaigns in which they participate.

The New York Times Interview

Peter Baker of *The New York Times* interviewed President Trump about his appointment of Jeff Sessions.

TRUMP: Look, Sessions gets the job. Right after he gets the job, he recuses himself.

BAKER: Was that a mistake?

TRUMP: Well, Sessions should have never recused himself, and if he was going to recuse himself, he should have told me before he took the job, and I would have picked somebody else. Jeff Sessions, the president's earliest and most fervent supporter in Congress, resigned under pressure as attorney general on Wednesday after brutal criticism from the president, bringing an abrupt end to his controversial tenure as the nation's top law enforcement officer.

Sessions noted in his resignation letter to the president that he was stepping down "at your request."

President Trump wrote on Twitter after a marathon press conference at the White House that Sessions was out and that Sessions' chief of staff, Matthew Whitaker, would serve as an acting replacement.

Sessions lasted not quite two years in the job. During this tumultuous period, he kept the Justice Department somewhat independent by recusing himself, and by standing up to the president. Sessions' recusal set the stage for Rod Rosenstein to appoint Robert Mueller as special counsel and to supervise his investigation. See Chapter Three.

The Appointment of William Barr

William Barr has become the best argument for the independent election of the attorney general. He has routinely represented the interests of President Trump and not of the nation. Donald B. Ayer, Former Deputy Attorney General under Republican President George H.W. Bush, summed it up in testimony he gave before the House Committee on the Judiciary on June 23, 2020: "I believe that Attorney General Barr is a major threat to our legal system and to public trust in it. That is because he does not believe in its central tenet–that no person is above the law. For the past sixteen months, he has been working hard to free the president from accountability under a broad range of checks and balances that have played a critical role in our system for many decades. He has also grossly misused his powers as Attorney General to advance the president's personal and political interests, and to protect his friends."

Confirmation Promises Unkept

When William Barr was appointed attorney general, critics warned that Barr would do everything he could to either interfere with Special Counsel Robert Mueller's work or suppress his report. In his confirmation hearings, Barr pledged to release as much of the report as he could under the law.

Barr failed to live up to his pledge because he failed to release as much of the report as he could. Barr was sneaky and clever. While making a summary of the report public, Barr managed to mislead the public and Congress, spinning Mueller's findings in a way that undercut their impact and protected the president.

The gap between Barr's statements and what Mueller actually concluded is obvious from any comparison of Barr's initial summary of conclusions to Congress, released March 24, and his April 18 pre-release press conference with the actual text of Mueller's report.

Mueller was outraged by Barr's handling of his report. In a letter to Barr on March 27, 2019, Mueller took issue, calmly but strenuously, with

Barr's public summary:

> The summary letter the Department sent
> to Congress and released to the public
> late in the afternoon of March 24 did not
> fully capture the context, nature, and

<blockquote>
substance of this Office's work and conclusion. . . There is now public confusion about critical aspects of the results of our investigation. This threatens to undermine a central purpose for which the Department appointed the Special Counsel: to assure full public confidence in the outcome of the investigations.
</blockquote>

Based on Barr's letter, immediate media reports portrayed Mueller as having found no collusion and no obstruction of justice. In fact, the report's findings on both of these questions were considerably more nuanced. Mueller avoided the non-legal term collusion, saying he found no criminal conspiracy, but he found considerable links between Donald Trump's campaign and Russia, and strongly suggested that Trump had obstructed justice, even while saying he didn't feel he could charge Trump.

Mueller was immediately worried in the days after Barr's "summary" was released. On March 25, he wrote, his team "communicated our concern to the Department." Apparently not receiving any satisfactory response, Mueller escalated his efforts, writing his letter to Barr on March 27th. Putting the complaint in writing formalized it. It also all but guaranteed that the letter would eventually make it to the public, as it now has. Lawyers are typically very careful about what they do and don't put in writing for precisely that reason, but throughout the Trump presidency, government officials have seen the need to write memos for posterity when concerned about actions by the administration.

Barr did not release the executive summaries prepared by the Mueller team, as Mueller wanted him to do, deciding to instead forge forward with releasing the full report and not the summaries. Barr said that he felt releasing parts of the report piecemeal would confuse the public. But that same critique could be leveled even more powerfully at his own, misleading-by-omission summary. And by releasing his own four-page letter, Barr sidestepped the pressure to immediately release the report's own summaries.

Barr then proceeded to give a baffling press conference on April 18, 2019, the morning the Mueller report was published. The press conference came before any member of Congress or the public had seen the report, and allowed Barr to once again frame the special counsel's report as he saw fit. For a second time, Barr offered a completely misleading view of what was in the report. Portraying Trump as the victim of the whole proceeding, he repeatedly stated that there was no "collusion," starting to sound like an echo of Trump's Twitter feed. Barr insisted that Trump had "fully cooperated with the special counsel's investigation." That claim was directly contradicted by the report itself, which pointed out multiple instances of the White House resisting cooperation, not least of them Trump's refusal to be interviewed by investigators or to answer written questions about obstructtion.

Even though Barr and Mueller are old friends and colleagues, they seem to be talking past each other in these exchanges. Clearly, the two men had differences of opinion about obstruction—Mueller implies he would have charged Trump were he not president, while Barr insists Mueller said otherwise in their conversations. Bill Barr said that he was surprised Mueller hedged on the obstruction question but felt that he needed to make a decision. But Mueller's letter doesn't object to Barr's decision or question his authority to make it. Mueller's problem was that Barr was misleading the public.

Chris Coons, a Delaware Democratic Senator, explained the importance during the hearing:

> A critical three weeks passed between when you delivered the letter with the focus on the principal conclusions and when we ultimately got the redacted report," Coons said. "My concern is that that gave President Trump and his folks more than three weeks of an open field to say, 'I was completely exonerated.'" As a way of defusing the findings of the investigation, it was tremendously successful. Even though the report can read

as an impeachment referral to Congress, by the time its full text was released, the ardor for impeachment hearings among legi-slators and the public had faded because of Barr's prejudicial statements under-mining Mueller's report.

U.S. District Judge Reggie Walton, and former Chief Judge of the Foreign Intelligence Surveillance Court, as well as a Republican appointee, noted in March, 2020, the Barr's conduct had "cause[d] the Court to seriously question whether Attorney General Barr made a calculated attempt to influence public discourse" in favor of President Trump contrary to the actual content of the report.

Judge Walton also noted that the redacted version of the Mueller Report released by William Barr included facts that were directly contrary to the sum-mary prepared by Barr. According to the redacted version of the Mueller Report, Special Counsel Mueller, "identified multiple contacts between Trump [c]ampaign officials and individuals with ties to the Russian government."

However, because coordination—the term that appears in the Appointment Order—"does not have a settled definition in federal criminal law," Special Counsel Mueller, "[i]n evaluating whether evidence about collective action of multiple individuals constituted a crime, applied the framework of conspiracy law," understanding

"coordination to require an agreement—tacit or express—between the Trump [c]ampaign and the Russian government on election interference," which "requires more than the two parties taking actions that were informed by or responsive to the other's actions or interests," and concluded that the investigation did not establish that "these contacts involved or resulted in coordination or a conspiracy with the Trump [c]ampaign and Russia, including with respect to Russia providing assistance to the [Trump] [c]am-paign in exchange for any sort of favorable treatment in the future."

Concerning obstruction of justice, Judge Walton ruled:

> With respect to Special Counsel Mueller's investigation into whether President Trump obstructed justice, Special Counsel Mueller accepted the Department's Office of Legal Counsel's legal conclusion " 'that the indictment or criminal prosecution of a sitting [p]resident would impermissibly undermine the capacity of the executive branch to perform its constitutionally assigned functions' in violation of the constitutional separation

of powers" for the purpose of exercising prosecutorial jurisdiction and "determined not to make a traditional prosecutorial judgment[,] . . . recogniz[ing] that a federal criminal accusation against a sitting [p]resident would place burdens on the [p]resident's capacity to govern and potentially preempt constitutional processes for addressing presidential misconduct."

Therefore, Barr's statement that there was "no collusion" and "no obstruction" was false and misleading to the public and to Congress.

There may not have been a conspiracy, but there undeniably was collusion. "Collusion," according to *Merriam-Webster*, means, "cooperation especially for an illegal or deceitful purpose." The Russians certainly cooperated with the Trump campaign, giving them dirt on Hillary Clinton, and thousands of stolen emails. In addition, there were more than 100 documents contacts between Trump campaign officials and Russian government agents. And further, the purpose was deceitful and illegal.

The Roger Stone Prosecution

Concerning the prosecution of Roger Stone, Attorney General Barr continued to represent the interests of the president, and not the American people or the Justice Department. In February, 2020, four assistant U.S. Attorneys recommended that Trump longtime crony Roger Stone be sentenced to from seven to nine years for lying to Congress and threatening a witness.

Stone, 67, has been a friend of Mr. Trump's for decades. He was convicted in November, 2019 of obstructing an inquiry by the House

Intelligence Committee into Russian interference in the 2016 election, in which Russia helped Trump get elected, lying to investigators under oath and trying to block the testimony of a witness who would have exposed his lies.

Trump immediately tweeted that he thought that that recommended sentence was too harsh. "Is this the Judge that put Paul Manafort in SOLITARY CONFINEMENT, something that not even mobster Al Capone had to endure? How did she treat Crooked Hillary Clinton? Just asking!" Trump tweeted that it was a "miscarriage of justice," according to a Justice Department spokeswoman. Mr. Trump said that Mr. Stone was treated "very badly," and that prosecutors "ought to apologize to him."

Barr responded to the implied directions of Trump's tweets and informed the court that the Justice Department did not support the sentence recommended by the Assistant U.S. Attorneys. President

Trump congratulated his attorney general on for intervening to lower the Justice Department's sentencing recommendation for the president's longtime friend.

The response of the U.S. attorneys handling the case was immediate. Jonathan Kravis was the first to resign, both from the case and as an assistant U.S. attorney. Kravis, a career DOJ prosecutor Kravis filed a motion to withdraw, announcing he had also resigned as an assistant

U.S. attorney. Kravis previously clerked for Judge Merrick Garland on the U.S. Court of Appeals for the D.C. Circuit and for Justice Stephen Breyer on the United States Supreme Court.

Jonathan Kravis was a federal prosecutor for ten years. Kravis said, "I resigned from the Justice Department after ten years as a career prosecutor. I left a job I loved because I believed the department had abandoned its responsibility to do justice in one of my cases, *United States v. Roger Stone*. At the time, I thought that the handling of the Stone case, with senior officials intervening to recommend a lower sentence for a longtime ally of President Trump, was a disastrous mistake that the department would not make again. I was wrong." (Kravis later criticized the Department's motion to dismiss the General Flynn prosecution.)

Kravis, said, "In February, the Justice Department filed a sentencing memorandum, signed by all four prosecutors in the case, recommending a sentence of seven to nine years, within the range set by the U.S. sentencing guidelines. In my experience, the Justice Department staunchly defends sentences within the guidelines range, particularly for defendants (such as Stone) who are convicted at trial, and especially for defendants (such as Stone) who repeatedly demonstrate disrespect for the judicial system."

The next morning, the president posted a tweet criticizing the sentencing recommendation as a "miscarriage of justice." Later that day, the Justice Department submitted a revised memo revoking the original recommendation and proposing that Stone receive a much shorter sentence.

Soon after, Aaron Zelinksy, the lead prosecutor on the case, notified the court that he was resigning "effective immediately" as a special prosecutor with the U.S. attorney's office in Washington, but would stay on as an assistant U.S. attorney in Baltimore. Zelinsky, who has spent the past three years working for Rod Rosenstein in Maryland as an assistant US attorney, was detailed to special counsel Robert Mueller's team. He clerked for Judge Thomas Griffith of the U.S. Court of Appeals for the DC Circuit.

Two of the prosecutors who resigned—Adam C. Jed and Aaron Zelinsky—began working on the case as members of the special counsel's team. Former Mueller prosecutor Adam Jed filed a notice of withdrawal. Jed is a Harvard Law School graduate and clerked for Supreme Court Justice John Paul Stevens. Michael

Marando, a Cornell law graduate, was the fourth prosecutor to resign.

All four of these prosecutors, with sterling credentials, resigned when Attorney General Barr interfered in the case as was suggested by President Trump.

Aaron Zelinsky testified before the House Judiciary Committee on

June 24, 2020. His testified:

> What I saw was the Department of Justice exerting significant pressure on the line prosecutors in the case to obscure the correct Sentencing Guidelines calculation to which Roger Stone was subject – and to water down and in some cases outright distort the events that transpired in his trial and the criminal conduct that gave rise to his conviction. Such pressure resulted in the virtually unprecedented decision to override the original sentencing recommendation in his case and to file a new sentencing memorandum that included statements and assertions at odds with the record and contrary to Department of Justice policy.

What I heard – repeatedly – was that Roger Stone was being treated differently from any other defendant because of his relationship to the President. I was told that the Acting U.S. Attorney for the District of Columbia, Timothy Shea, was receiving heavy pressure from the highest levels of the Department of Justice to cut Stone a break, and that the U.S. Attorney's sentencing instructions to us were based on political considerations. I was also told that the acting U.S. Attorney was giving Stone such unprecedentedly favorable treatment because he was "afraid of the President."

That explanation was deeply unsettling. Together with my fellow line Assistant United States Attorneys, I immediately and repeatedly raised concerns, in writing and orally, that such political favoritism was wrong and contrary to legal ethics and Department policy.

Our objections were not heeded. When I learned that the Department was going to issue a new sentencing memo, I made the difficult decision to resign from the case.

                    *   *   *

Roger Stone is a longtime friend and associate of President Trump. In the summer of 2016, Stone was considered by the Trump campaign to be the campaign's access point to WikiLeaks.

Throughout the summer and fall, Stone was in regular contact with the highest levels of the Trump campaign, which was relying on him for information about Wikileaks's activities.

Beginning in spring 2016, Stone told senior Trump campaign officials that he had inside knowledge regarding Wiki-Leaks's plans, and that he communicated with Julian Assange. Stone made these claims throughout the summer to Deputy Campaign Chairman Rick Gates, Campaign Chairman Paul Manafort, and Campaign CEO Steve Bannon. These men believed his claims, and they sought information from Stone about what WikiLeaks would do to help the Trump campaign. Moreover, as the summer wore on, the senior leadership found Stone's predictions to be reliable. Manafort instructed Gates to keep in touch with Stone regarding WikiLeaks so that he could keep then-candidate Trump updated on Stone's information. And the senior level of the Trump campaign began brainstorming a press strategy based in part on Stone's predictions of a WikiLeaks release of documents that would be damaging to the Clinton campaign.

That summer, Stone reached out to both Manafort and Bannon, telling Manafort that
Stone had a "plan to save Trump's ass." And in August 2016, Stone told Bannon he knew how to "win but this ain't pretty." Bannon responded, "let's talk ASAP." During this same time period, Stone also publicly bragged that he had a backchannel to Julian Assange, and "therefore I am a recipient of pretty good information."

On Friday, October 7, 2016, WikiLeaks began dumping into the public domain thousands of emails which the Russian government had hacked from Clinton campaign Chairman John Podesta's personal email account. Minutes after Wiki-

Leaks began releasing the hacked emails, one of Trump campaign CEO Bannon's aides texted Stone, "well done." That weekend, Campaign CEO Steve Bannon himself heard that Stone was involved in the WikiLeaks release of the hacked emails.

And that summer, Stone wasn't just talking to the CEO, Chairman, and Deputy Chairman of the campaign. He was talking directly to then-candidate Trump himself.

On June 14, 2016, the Democratic National Committee (DNC) announced that it had been hacked earlier that spring by the Russian Government. That evening, Stone called Trump, and they spoke on Trump's personal line. We don't know what they said. On July 31, Stone again called then-candidate Trump, and the two spoke for approximately ten minutes. Again, we don't know what was said, but less than an hour after speaking with Trump, Stone emailed an associate of his, Jerome Corsi, to have someone else who was living in London "see Assange."

Less than two days later, on August 2, 2016, Corsi emailed Stone. Corsi told Stone that, "Word is friend in embassy [Assange] plans 2 more dumps. One "in October" and that "impact planned to be very damaging," "time to let more than Podesta to be exposed as in bed w enemy if they are not ready to drop HRC. That appears to be the game hackers are now about."

* * *

President Trump criticized "flipping" witnesses and stated that Stone was "very brave" in indicating he would not co-operate with prosecutors. The Special Counsel's Report stated that the President's statements complimenting Stone "support the inference that the President intended to communicate a message that witnesses could be rewarded for refusing to provide testimony adverse to the President."

The Michael Flynn Prosecution

Lieutenant General Michael Flynn became a senior advisor to President Trump during his presidential campaign and served as the National Security Advisor from January 23 to February 13, 2017.

Special Counsel Robert Mueller investigated Flynn's involvement in the Trump Administrations relationship with Russian leadership. This investigation led to charges being brought against General Flynn.

On December 1, 2017, Flynn appeared in federal court and formalized a plea deal with Special Counsel Robert Mueller. Flynn agreed to plead guilty to a felony count of "willfully and knowingly" making "false, fictitious and fraudulent statements" to the FBI. He also agreed to cooperate with the Special Counsel's investigation.

Flynn initially admitted to urging Russian Ambassador Sergey Kislyak not to respond by escalating the Obama administration's December, 2016 sanctions on Moscow for interfering in the U.S. presidential election. After that call, Russia said it would not impose any retaliatory sanctions.

Flynn also confessed that he falsely told investigators he had not discussed Russia's response to the sanctions with Kislyak.

After Mr. Barr became Attorney General he acceded to Trump's desire to get Flynn off the hook. Trump considered pardoning Flynn, but found that Barr had an easier, less politically damaging route, to get the charges against Flynn dropped. Barr installed his close associate Timothy Shea as U.S. Attorney for the District of Columbia. Fox News described

Shea as Barr's "right-hand man" at the Justice Department. Before Flynn's sentencing, Shea filed a motion to dismiss the case against Flynn, a highly unusual reversal of course by the Justice Department. The career prosecutor assigned to the Flynn case while working in Mueller's office, Brandon van Grack, withdrew, and the department's notice to Judge Sullivan was signed only by the top prosecutor for Washington, DC.

Shea was appointed in January, 2020 after Trump nominated former U.S. attorney for D.C. Jessie Liu— who oversaw the prosecutions of Flynn, Roger Stone, Paul Manafort and other spinoffs from the Mueller investigation — to serve in a top Treasury Department role.

Trump abruptly withdrew Liu's nomination for the treasury role in February after reviewing one of the "Deep State" memos compiled by conservative activists about allegedly disloyal government officials.

Former federal prosecutor Kravis said, "in May, 2020, came an equally appalling chapter: the department's motion to drop the Flynn case. Flynn pleaded guilty to the crime of making false statements in connection with lies he told in an FBI interview about his contacts with the Russian ambassador. Flynn twice admitted under oath that he had committed this crime, and the trial judge issued a lengthy opinion upholding the plea. Nevertheless, after public criticism of the prosecution by the president, the department moved to dismiss Flynn's case, claiming that new evidence showed that the plea had no basis. None of the career prosecutors who handled Flynn's case signed that motion."

House Judiciary Chairman Jerry Nadler (D-N.Y.) tweeted: "This is outrageous! Flynn PLEADED GUILTY to lying to investigators. The evidence against him is overwhelming. Now, a politicized DOJ is dropping the case. The decision to overrule the special counsel is without precedent and warrants an immediate explanation."

House Intelligence Committee Chairman Adam Schiff said, "Flynn pled guilty to lying to the FBI about illicit Russian contacts. His lies do not now become truths. This dismissal does not exonerate him. But it does incriminate Bill Barr. In the worst politicization of the Justice Department in its history.

The *New York Times* wrote an editorial entitled, "William Barr's Perversion of Justice." May 9, 2020. *The Times* said, "The attorney general is turning the Justice Department into a political weapon for the president. In service to Mr. Trump, Mr. Barr is abusing his power not to write, but to erase, some of the most important lessons of American history."

The *Times* editorial board noted, "The Watergate scandal, with its revelations of how dangerous a renegade White House could be, led to reforms meant to ensure **an independent Justice Department,** one faithful to the law rather than to the Oval Office. Those reforms have not be effective. The Department of Justice and the attorney general are still captives of the occupant of the White House."

"Bill Barr's America is not a place that anyone, including Trump voters, should want to go," **wrote Donald Ayer,** who served as deputy attorney general under the first President Bush. "It is a banana republic where all are subject to the whims of a dictatorial president and his henchmen."

The Times continued, "Bill Barr's America is the one we're now living in. The Justice Department, in the midst of a presidential campaign, has become a political weapon. Having absorbed the lessons of Watergate, mainstream Republicans once balked at the politicization of the Justice Department — even by Republican presidents. But today's Republicans, who could be most effective in defending the integrity of American justice, appear either too afraid of Mr. Trump or too eager for short-term partisan advantage to confront the danger to the country.

Mr. Barr's decision to drop the charges against Mr. Flynn may be his most egregious abandonment of his role as the public's lawyer, but it's certainly not the first. Last year, barely a month after he was confirmed to his post, he stood before the American people and misrepresented the contents of the long-awaited report by Robert Mueller, the special counsel who investigated ties between the Trump campaign and the Russian government in 2016."

Southern District of New York

The United States Attorney for the Southern District of New York is one of the most powerful federal attorney's offices in the country. It is often known as the U.S. Attorney for the Sovereign District of New York because of its well-known independence from Washington.

The Manhattan office prosecuted President Trump's former attorney Michael Cohen for his mishandling of the President's illegal campaign payments to porn star Stormy Daniels and Playboy Playmate of the Month Karen McDougal. American Media, Inc., the owner of the *National Enquirer*, had paid McDougal $150,000 for exclusive rights to her story, but never published it.

In August, 2018, Cohen pleaded guilty to breaking campaign finance laws, admitting paying hush money of $130,000 and $150,000 "at the direction of a candidate for federal office" to two women who alleged affairs with that candidate, "with the purpose of influencing the election." These figures match payments made to adult film actress Stormy Daniels and

McDougal. Daniels has also alleged a 2006 affair with Trump while he was married to First Lady Melania Trump.

David Pecker was the publisher of the National Enquirer, and a close friend of President Trump. In 2018, Pecker became embroiled in controversy regarding his involvement in a catch and kill operation to buy exclusive rights to stories that might embarrass his friend Donald Trump, to prevent the stories from becoming public during the 2016 presidential campaign. In 2019, former Trump lawyer Michael Cohen stated that he assisted Pecker in this operation. Federal investigators subpoenaed Pecker and American Media in April, 2018, with Pecker providing prosecutors details about the hush payments Cohen had arranged. In August of 2018, Pecker was granted witness immunity in exchange for his testimony of Trump's knowledge of the payments.

Federal prosecutors from the SDNY contended that the Trump Organization had improperly booked reimbursements for the hush-money scheme as "legal expenses," with the aid of sham invoices. They granted legal immunity to Trump Organization CFO Allen Weisselberg, a 72-yearold accountant running the Trump's business with Trump's two adult sons. Prosecutors later closed their 18-month investigation with the guilty plea of Michael Cohen.

Cohen was sentenced to three years in prison but served only a year. He was released early because of the Covid epidemic that was spreading in many prisons.

Cyrus Vance, Manhattan's District Attorney, picked up the ball and his state grand jury is examining whether Weisselberg, among others—including the Trump Organization—should face state criminal charges for falsification of business records, according to *Pro Publica.*

The Southern District was also investigating President Trump's personal attorney, Rudolph Guiliani. Giuliani was under investigation for a wide range of possible crimes by the same office he led from 1983 to 1989. In October, 2019, Southern District prosecutors charged two of Giuliani's associates, Lev Parnas and Igor Fruman, with campaign-finance crimes. Investigators have expanded their inquiry to include Giuliani. Authorities are examining his business dealings with the Soviet-born men in Ukraine, and FBI agents and prosecutors have questioned witnesses about their potential or actual business arrangements with Giuliani, his work on the ground in Ukraine and the identities of his clients.

Parnas and Fruman pleaded not guilty to the charges in which federal prosecutors accuse the pair of funneling foreign money illegally into U.S. politics and violating other campaign finance laws. John Dowd, who was formerly a personal attorney for Trump, is representing Parnas and Fruman.

When these two associates of President Trump's personal lawyer, Rudy Giuliani, were arrested at Dulles airport this outside of Washington, D.C. on October 9, 2019, for campaign finance violations, it wasn't immediately clear how — or even if — those activities were related to the impeachment inquiry into Trump. The House of Representatives began investigating the impeachment of President Trump in September of that year for Trump's blackmailing of Ukraine's President Zelensky by withholding arms until he gave Trump information on former Vice President Biden.

Over the past two years, the Ukrainian businessmen crossed paths repeatedly with people and events at the center of the impeachment inquiry, both in the U.S. and in the Ukraine. Trevor Potter is a Republican who used to chair the Federal Election Commission. (I worked as an attorney for the Federal Election Commission under Mr. Potter.) He also served as general counsel for John McCain's 2000 and 2008 presidential campaigns. Potter runs a group called the Campaign Legal Center. His team scans political contributions, looking for suspicious trans-actions that it reports to authorities.

The Campaign Legal Center found out that Global Energy Producers gave $325,000 to America First Action, the superPAC supporting Trump. When Potter and his team started digging into the company that made the contribution, they found that "it was a blank slate."

"The company hadn't existed. It had been formed literally a couple weeks before the contribution," Potter noted. "It had no website, no history of political activity, so you're thinking this is most likely a company created to make this contribution." Setting up a shell company to hide a political contribution — is illegal.

"You have to disclose on the FEC reports the true source of the money, who the contributor actually is," Potter explained. Potter and his team wanted to know who was behind the company.

So they kept digging and found addresses associated with Global Energy Producers—in South Florida and New York. They found contributions to Pete Sessions of Texas, who was a Republican congressman at the time but lost his reelection bid in 2018. The donors were Lev Parnas and Igor Fruman. In July, 2018, Potter's group alerted the FEC about possible campaign violations by Parnas and Fruman.

The SDNY had been examining the Turkish bank Halkbank for allegedly violating U.S. sanctions against Iran. John Bolton, Trump's former National Security Advisor told ABC's Martha Raddatz that Trump's suggestion of getting involved in the investigation of the Turkish bank felt like "obstruction of justice to me." Bolton asserted that Trump and Turkish President

Recep Tayyip Erdoğan had discussed the investigation several times, with the Turkish president seeking a settlement for Halkbank.

President Trump fired Geoffrey Berman, the federal prosecutor whose office put his former personal lawyer in prison and is investigating his current one, heightening criticism that the president was carrying out an extraordinary purge to rid his administration of officials whose independence could be a threat to his re-election campaign.

Mr. Trump's dismissal of the United States attorney in Manhattan, whose office has pursued one case after another that have rankled Mr. Trump, led to political blowback and an unexpected result: By the end of the day, Mr. Berman's handpicked deputy, not the administration's favored replacement, was chosen to succeed him for now.

The abrupt ouster of Mr. Berman came as Mr. Trump sought to reinvigorate his campaign with its first public rally in months and days after new allegations by John Bolton, his former national security adviser that he had engaged in "obstruction of justice as a way of life."

The President wanted to install his close associate, Jay Clayton, to the Southern District post. The most prominent critic of the move was Senator Lindsey Graham, Republican of South Carolina and a close ally of the president's. Mr. Graham, chairman of the Senate Judiciary Committee, suggested in a statement that he would allow New York's two Democratic senators to thwart the nomination through a procedural maneuver.

The Southern District has also been investigating irregularities with the Trump Inaugural Committee. President Trump's inaugural committee received a sweeping subpoena from the Southern District of New York. The scope of documents requested in the subpoena and potential crimes investigators are probing everything from false statements to money laundering. Investigators are said to be interested in the inaugural committee's spending, its donations, whether any donations came from illegal foreign sources, and potential corruption involving favors for donors.

Trump's inaugural committee raised a truly astonishing $106.7 million, double the previous record set by Barack Obama's 2009 inaugural. There have been many questions about where that money came from, and where it went.

Rick Gates, the former Trump campaign aide who helped run the inaugural committee and struck a plea deal with Mueller in February, 2018. On December 17, 2019, Gates was sentenced to three years of probation, 45 days in jail, and 300 hours of community service. He was also ordered to pay a $20,000 fine. The judge took into account years of financial crimes and deception that continued even after he had agreed to plead guilty and cooperate.

The *Wall Street Journal* reported that Gates had also been cooperating with SDNY prosecutors.

The *Wall Street Journal* reported that the documents the Southern District demanded from the inaugural committee include:

- "All documents related to the committee's donors and vendors"

- All records related to "benefits" provided to donors

- Documents related to the financier Imaad Zuberi and his company Avenue Ventures LLC. (He is the only donor specifically named in the subpoena.)

- Documents related to donations "made by or on behalf of foreign nationals," including communications about possible donations from foreign individuals.

- Documents related to "donations or payments made by donors directly to contractors and/or vendors."

CNN reported that the subpoena specifically named several different offenses that investigators are probing:

- Conspiracy against the United States

- False statements

- Mail fraud

- Wire fraud

- Money laundering

- Inaugural committee disclosure violations

- "Violations of laws prohibiting contributions by foreign nations and contributions in the name of another person, also known as straw donors."

-

The Trump inaugural committee was chaired by billionaire real estate investor Tom Barrack, a long-time close friend of Trump. Barrack turned to Rick Gates—Paul Manafort's right-hand man, who remained on the Trump campaign after Manafort was fired—to handle much of the fundraising and planning work.

Mueller indicted Gates for financial and lobbying crimes connected to his work with Manafort. Gates reportedly provided information about the Trump inauguration to SDNY investigators.

Imaad Zuberi, a California venture capitalist who was a major donor for Democrats before shifting the most of his donations to

Republicans after the 2016 election, was charged by prosecutors in the Southern District of New York with obstructing a federal investigation into donations to President Trump's inaugural committee. Zuberi, had pleaded guilty last year to separate charges brought by federal prosecutors in Los Angeles related to earlier campaign donations, as well as lobbying and tax violations. He is expected to plead guilty to the obstruction charge as well.

The obstruction charge stemmed from a federal investigation into the source of the $900,000 Mr. Zuberi donated through his company, Avenue Ventures, to Mr. Trump's inaugural committee in late December 2016.

The Southern District of New York is prosecuting and investi-gating many of Trump's associates, including his attorney, Rudolph Guiliani, the inaug-ural committee and the Trump Organization. It seems clear that President Trump wanted to stop these investigations and install his own person as U.S. attorney.

Attorney General Barr's move to remove the Man-hattan U.S. Attorney was clearly political and made for the personal benefit of President Trump. Barr clearly has been acted more as Trump's personal attorney than as the chief attorney for the United States of America.

Bring on the Army

The abuse of Barr's power in support of Trump's campaign efforts that has shocked the public conscience has been his role in directing law enforcement forces on June 1, 2020 to violate the First Amendment rights of peaceful protestors by forcibly clearing them out of Lafayette Park and making way to stage a media event with the President holding a Bible for pictures in front of St. John's Church.

Barr personally marched with the president, surrounded by military forces, across Lafayette Park after teargas and rubber bullets parted the protesters. The officers present with Barr included many from parts of the Department of Justice–including the FBI, the Bureau of Prisons, the
Bureau of Alcohol Tobacco and Firearms, and the Drug Enforcement Administration. The disturbing events of that evening unleashed a wave of outrage from Generals James Mattis and John Kelly, Colin Powell, and others. Barr has disputed the evidence that demonstrators conduct that night was peaceful, and echoed the president's unsupported assertions blaming "Antifa" for violent behavior while making no mention of the presence of violent right-wing groups. He also denied that he ordered the enforcement action in order to facilitate a photo opportunity– even though it occurred just minutes before the President walked

across the square—and argued about the difference between pepper balls and tear gas, at least the first of which was undeniably used by police.

On June 10, 2020 more than 1,250 former Justice Department workers called on the agency's Inspector General to investigate Attorney General William P. Barr's involvement in law enforcement's move last week to push a crowd of largely peaceful demonstrators back from Lafayette Square using horses and gas.

In a letter to Justice Department's Inspector General Michael Horowitz, the group said it was "deeply concerned about the Department's actions, and those of Attorney General William Barr himself, in response to the nationwide lawful gatherings to protest the systemic racism that has plagued this country throughout its history."

"In particular, we are disturbed by Attorney General Barr's possible role in ordering law enforcement personnel to suppress a peaceful do-mestic protest in Lafayette Square on June 1, 2020, for the purpose of enabling President Trump to walk across the street from the White House and stage a photo op at St. John's Church, a politically motivated event in which Attorney General Barr participated," the group wrote.

The group of career DOJ prosecutors asked Horowitz to "immediately open and conduct an investigation of the full scope of the Attorney General's and the DOJ's role" in that and other events. "The rule of law, the maintenance of the Department's integrity, and the very safety of our citizens demand nothing less," the group wrote. The signatories are mostly former career prosecutors, supervisors and trial lawyers who are not household names and worked in both Republican and Democratic administrations. The letter was organ-ized by the nonprofit group Protect Demo-cracy, which has sent similar demands in the past calling on Barr to resign and asserting that Trump would have been charged with obstructing special counsel Robert S. Mueller's probe had the Justice Department's Office of Legal Counsel not ruled that presidents cannot be indicted while in office.

Stonewalling Oversight

President Trump's total stonewalling of congress's traditional oversight power, normally exercised through subpoenaing documents and calling wit-nesses, has only been possible with the complicity of the Department of Justice. Barr's prior opinions as the head of the Office of Legal Counsel have played a prominent role in providing "authority" for new opinions issued by Barr's OLC to support many of his current initiatives.

These outrageous assertions include the idea that executive branch officials need not raise a specific claim of executive privilege with regard to particular information, but rather can simply assert a sweeping absolute immunity claim that excuses their need even to appear or raise any specific objection.

The Department of Justice has also stonewalled, so far successfully, the House Ways and Means Committee's request to the Treasury Department to turn over the President's tax returns, despite a statute that requires the Treasury to do so. And in a case now pending before the Supreme Court, this claim of immunity from any obligation of transparency is asserted to include a sweeping absolute immunity from process issued by State grand juries to investigate crimes under their laws, for records in the hands of a third party reflecting the President's personal affairs.

In September, 2019, the Office of Legal Counsel issued an opinion directing the Inspector General for the Intelligence Community that the whistleblower complaint relating to the June, 2019 phone call between President Trump and the president of Ukraine was not a matter of urgent concern that was required by statute to be referred to the House Intelligence Committee. That ridiculous conclusion was met by a letter of stern rebuke from the entire Federal inspector general community. When Trump fired that same IG in April, 2020, apparently just for doing his job, Barr spoke up publicly to endorse the action as justified.

The Appointment of Pam Bondi

President Trump's appointment of Pam Bondi as attorney general at the start of his second term, demonstrates why the attorney general should be independently elected. She serves Trump's personal interests. Bondi is using the Justice Department to go after Trump's personal enemies.

Bondi said in a recent cabinet meeting that Trump, "was overwhelmingly elected by the biggest majority." In fact, according to the American Presidency Project at the University of California at Santa Barbara, President Trump only won by 1.4% and did not even receive a majority of the votes cast. This clearly is not an overwhelming victory and certainly not the biggest majority.

Pam Bondi has been a very committed Trump loyalist through even his most flagrantly lawless moments. *Politico* reported that just after Trump lost reelection in 2020, Bondi immediately joined forces with Rudy Giuliani to sow doubts about the results, helping lay the groundwork for his insurrection attempt. Bondi also stood by him when he faced prosecution for his criminal hush-money scheme and impeachment for extorting Vladimir Zelensky, President of the Ukraine.

Hours after she was sworn in at the White House, Bondi called for the creation of "weaponization working group" that will scrutinize the work of special counsel Jack Smith, who charged Trump in two criminal cases. The group will also review "unethical prosecutions" stemming from the Jan. 6, 2021, riot at the U.S. Capitol, among other things, according to the memo.

The memo satisfied the longstanding contention of Trump and his allies that the Justice Department under the Biden administration had become "weaponized" against conservatives, even though some of its most high-profile probes concerned the Democratic president and his son, and there's been no evidence to support the idea that the prosecutions against Trump were launched for a partisan purpose.

This was one of 14 directives signed by Bondi designed to roll back Biden administration policies and align the Justice Department with the priorities of a White House determined to exert control over federal law enforcement and purge agencies of career employees it views as disloyal.

One astonishing memo, exposed by *Slate*, puts the DOJ at the center of President Donald Trump's widespread efforts to destroy any traces of initiatives that would create inclusive and diverse workspaces, otherwise known as DEIA. The new memo claims that it will target private-sector diversity, equity, inclusion, and accessibility initiatives for potential "criminal investigation."

"The attorney general will be the weaponizer in chief of the legal system for Trump," Representative

Jamie Raskin, Democrat of Maryland, said of Bondi's appointment. Trump has threatened to prosecute enemies without cause, including all Justice Department attorneys who worked on the two cases against him.

During her stint as Florida attorney general, Bondi engaged in questionable practices—such as refraining from joining a lawsuit against Trump University. In 2013, Bondi's office received complaints from people alleging they had been scammed by Donald Trump's Trump University seminars. Florida did not pursue the case and Bondi's political committee received a $25000 donation from Donald Trump's foundation. At that time both Trump and Bondi denied any donation and link to that.

David Cay Johnston, Rochester Institute of Technology law professor commented, "Pam Bondi, Trump's new AG pick, is so corrupt. She took an illegal $25,000 campaign donation from the Trump Foundation. Bondi kept the money (!!!), given when—as Florida Attorney General—she shut down her office's investigation of the utterly fraudulent Trump University."

Mayor Eric Adams and Jeffrey Epstein

The DOJ's move to scuttle the case against Eric Adams followed months of Mayor Adams refusing to go after Trump and expressing a willingness to work with him. The New York mayor also met with Trump at the president's Palm Beach golf course a few days before he took office and attended Trump's inauguration at the last minute.

Dale Ho, the federal judge who threw out Adams' case, stated in his ruling that it appeared that the mayor's attorney traded his cooperation for implementing Trump's immigration agenda for the president to drop his charges. Ho wrote: "Everything here smacks of a bargain: dismissal of the Indictment in exchange for immigration policy concessions."

After the Justice Department filed a motion to dismiss Adams' case, he has met and appeared on television with Trump's "Border Czar" Tom Homan and pledged to issue an executive order allowing federal immigration authorities to operate on Rikers Island once again.

"The same Pam Bondi who let Jeffrey Epstein slide," Democrat strategist Ameshia Cross posted after Donald Trump named her as the attorney general. "If you ever wonder how Jeffrey Epstein was able to walk the Earth unprosecuted and have all of his contacts sealed, look no farther than Pam Bondi. Pam Bondi is the reason Jeffrey Epstein, and all of his information is sealed in the state of Florida," one post read. No one in elective office shielded Jeffrey Epstein more than Pam Bondi. Senate Judiciary Democrats' X account drew attention to Bondi's sidelining of Andrew Rohrbach, a prosecutor who worked on the federal cases against

New York Mayor Eric Adams and Epstein associate Ghislaine Maxwell.

"Pam Bondi just put the attorney who successfully prosecuted Ghislaine Maxwell ON LEAVE," the account posted. It quoted a thread from the previous week that highlighted Trump's relationships with Epstein.

Two Manhattan prosecutors who worked on the corruption case against New York City's mayor, Eric Adams, were put on administrative leave by the Justice Department, according to four people with knowledge of the matter.

The prosecutors, Celia Cohen and Andrew Rohrbach, had been serving in high-ranking positions in the U.S. attorney's office for the Southern District of New York. Ms. Cohen had been chief counsel to the acting U.S. attorney, Matthew Podolsky, while Mr. Rohrbach had worked as a co-chief of the general crimes unit.

Three of the people said the Justice Department in Washington had acted without any warning. Ms. Cohen and Mr. Rohrbach were given letters signed by Todd Blanche, the deputy attorney general, notifying them they had been placed on leave. They were then immediately escorted out of the Lower Manhattan building that houses the U.S. attorney's office.

Targeting Law Firms

On March 22, 2025, President Donald Trump increased his threats against the American legal system, directing Attorney General Pam Bondi to take action against lawyers and law firms that go against him. Trump directed Bondi to seek sanctions against lawyers and law firms that "engage in frivolous, unreasonable, and vexatious litigation against the United States." Trump's administration has taken an increasingly adversarial stance toward the legal system, including both judges who have ruled against his policies and lawyers and firms that he has viewed as wronging him.

President Trump signed memorandums and orders that have targeted firms Covington & Burling; Jenner & Block; Paul, Weiss, Rifkind, Wharton & Garrison (Paul Weiss); Perkins Coie; Susman Godfrey (Susman); and Wilmer Cutler Pickering Hale and Dorr (WilmerHale). Trump's memorandums and orders also specifically targeted lawyers Marc Elias, Peter Koski, Jack Smith, Andrew Weissmann, Mark Pomerantz, James Quarles, Mark Zaid, Andrew Weissmann, Mark Zaid and Aaron Zebley.

The Trump administration made efforts to influence practices by law firms, including directing the Equal Employment Opportunity Commission (EEOC) to send letters to 20 law firms demanding information about each's Diversity, Equity and Inclusion (DEI) employment practices. The administration also threatened to bring attorneys before disciplinary proceedings, while individuals close to the administration campaign to become officials of the District of Columbia Bar, who would then oversee those proceedings for many of the attorneys.

Legal experts have stated that this targeting of law firms "could cast a chill over the freedom held by lawyers to represent clients of their choice." Law firms have responded in a variety of ways, with three firms—Jenner & Block, Perkins Coie, and WilmerHale—suing, and four firms—Milbank LLP; Paul Weiss; Skadden, Arps, Slate, Meagher & Flom (Skadden); and Willkie Farr & Gallagher (Willkie)—making deals with the Trump administration to obviate sanctions and restore access.

Claire Finkelstein, a law professor at the University of Pennsylvania, said the goal of these executive orders was to "intimidate professionals, to intimidate the legal profession from engaging in professional activities that go against Donald Trump and the current administration."

An anonymous attorney at a big law firm stated: "The president and those closest to him know that they have the ability to put more than a squeeze—a crush—on law firms, who have lawyers who speak out, advocate, organize, represent in a way which is unpleasant, undesirable for the administration...So lawyers and law firms are wanting to keep their head down and represent as small a target as they possibly can be...The financial implications for a law firm can be nuclear, and therefore it's a declaration of war against lawyers and law firms who have in some way offended somebody in the administration...The concerns of the law firms are legitimate. They're not imagined from the perspective of a law firm and its management. They have mouths to feed. They have families of lawyers and paralegals and secretaries and messengers that have to be taken into account. And so it's not as though it's an easy call —it's a painful call."

Another anonymous attorney said "Every lawyer now who litigates on behalf of a client against the administration, against an agency, against some executive action, against some agency action, against some law enforcement action has to now run the risk of being quote, unquote, sanctioned by the Department of Justice. I mean, we're talking Mussolini here."

University of California, Los Angeles law professor Scott Cummings and a former senior Justice Department official have both called Trump's moves attacking law firms and targeting lawyers "authoritarian." Senior American Civil Liberties Union attorney Ben Wizner said Trump's threats are an attempt to "chill and intimidate" lawyers who challenge him. In remarks delivered with the Governor of Louisiana, President Trump told reporters that he thinks "The law firms have to behave themselves, and we've proven that."

The American Bar Association released a statement encouraging everyone in the profession to stand up against the Trump's "efforts to undermine the courts and the legal profession," following that with another statement joined by over 50 smaller bar associations across the country.

The deans of nearly 80 law schools from across the country also signed a joint letter condemning the administration's actions, stating that "Punishing lawyers for their representation and advocacy violates the First Amendment and undermines the Sixth Amendment." Democratic state attorneys general sent a joint letter as well, condemning Trump's attempts to undermine the rule of law.

Eighty-two law school professors of Harvard Law School's 118 active professors signed an open letter condemning the Trump administration's actions against law firms law firms and lawyers under the second Trump administration Harvard Crimson, March 29, 2025.

After Skadden approached the Trump administration to reach an agreement before being targeted with an executive order, two other associates resigned, Brenna Trout Frey and Thomas Sipp. Trout Frey characterized the agreement as "a craven attempt to sacrifice the rule of law for self-preservation," and added that "if my employer cannot stand up for the rule of law, then I cannot ethically continue to work for them." She encouraged her colleagues to join her. Sipp said that "we are sliding into an autocracy where those in power are above the rule of law. . . . Skadden is on the wrong side of history. I could no longer stay knowing that someday I would have to explain why I stayed." Scores of alumni from both Skadden and Paul Weiss have signed open letters condemning their choice to agree to Trump's terms, expressing disappointment and outrage. The letter from the Paul Weiss alumni stated, "Instead of a ringing defense of the values of democracy, we witnessed a craven surrender to, and thus complicity in, what is perhaps the gravest threat to the independence of the legal profession since at least the days of Senator Joseph McCarthy."

Rachel Cohen, an associate at Skadden, organized an open letter in mid-March, inviting other associates to sign on. The letter, addressed to large law firms, called on them to take a stand. As of March 27, 2025, over 1,500 associates had signed it. On March 21, Cohen also submitted a conditional resignation letter, urging Skadden to fight Trump's actions; instead, they locked her out of their systems the same day. Cohen called the administration's actions an "existential" risk to the matter of law, stating that firms need to be united in condemnation, and that lawyers in "the upper echelons of a legal system in the United States—they have an obligation to protect that legal system itself."

Karoline Leavitt, the White House press secretary told *The New York Times*: "Big Law continues to bend the knee to President Trump because they know they were wrong, and he looks forward to putting their pro bono legal concessions toward implementing his America First agenda."

On April 8, 2025, Donald Trump commented on the situation by stating "Have you noticed that lots of law firms have been signing up with Trump? $100 million, another $100 million for, uh, damages that they've done. They give you $100 million and then they announce that, 'But we have done nothing wrong.' And I agree, they've done nothing wrong. But what the hell, they give me a lot of money considering they've done nothing wrong."

These scandals are prime examples of why the attorney general should be independent of the President of the United States. Michael R. Bromwich, who served the department's inspector general under President Bill Clinton, advised prosecutors to report all instances of improper political influence to the agency's watchdog. "This is not what you signed up for. The four prosecutors who bailed on the Stone case have shown the way," he wrote on Twitter. He described the political pressure from the White House as "truly a cancer on our system of justice."

More that 2,000 former federal prosecutors publicly criticized the decisions that Barr to undercut prosecution in the Roger Stone and Michael Flynn Prosecutions. Their open letter called for Attorney General Barr to resign:

We, the undersigned, are alumni of the United States Department of Justice (DOJ) who have collectively served both Republican and Democratic administrations. Each of us proudly took an oath to defend the Constitution and pursue the evenhanded administration of justice free from partisan consideration.

Many of us have spoken out previously to condemn President Trump's and Attorney General Barr's political interference in the Department's law enforcement decisions, as we did when Attorney General Barr overruled the sentencing recommendation of career prosecutors to seek favorable treatment for Roger Stone and Michael Flynn.

These brave former federal prosecutors have summarized the arguments for making the Department of Justice and the Attorney General independent of the President of the United States. The best way to accomplish this is to make the office of the attorney general an elected position and not an appointed one.

Bondi is more dedicated to President Trump than General Barr was. She has cast aside all claims of independence of the Justice Department and has become counsel for the President and not the country.

The Resignation of Attorney General Barr

Attorney General William Barr resigned after President Trump lost his re-election bid. But Barr's relationship with the president had become strained in recent weeks over the attorney general's refusal to back Trump's claims of widespread voter fraud in the 2020 election. Barr, contradicting Trump, said earlier in December stating that there was no evidence of "fraud on a scale that could have effected a different outcome in the election." Barr had reportedly told associates in recent weeks that he was considering stepping down from his post before Inauguration Day.

Trump retweeted a post that called for Barr to be fired. Trump also added his own commentary: "A big disappointment!"

Barr's admission that there was no fraud during an interview with the Associated Press undercut the president, who has refused to concede to Biden and is falsely claiming he won the election, citing an array of unproven fraud conspiracies and asserting the race was "rigged" against him.

The statements from Barr also sharply undermined the legal efforts from lawyers on the Trump campaign to reverse Biden's wins in key swing states.

Jeffrey Rosen

On February 19, 2019, President Donald Trump announced his intention to nominate Rosen for the position of United States Deputy Attorney General, succeeding Rod Rosenstein upon his departure from the Department of Justice. His nomination to become the second-highest law enforcement official was unusual, as Rosen had no previous prosecutorial experience. Attorney General William Barr had urged Trump to choose Rosen as his deputy. Rosen was sworn in on May 22, 2019.

In June 2019, Rosen sent a letter to New York state prosecutors inquiring into the case of Paul Manafort and indicating that he would be monitoring where Manafort would be held in custody. Shortly thereafter, federal prison officials informed New York state prosecutors that Manafort would not be held in Rikers Island. Current and former prosecutors described this decision as unusual, because most individuals held in custody while awaiting federal trial are held in Rikers Island, a prison with a reputation for violence and mismanagement.

In late 2019, Rosen stalled a probe of former Department of Interior head Ryan Zinke. Federal prosecutors proposed to move forward with possible criminal charges against Zinke over his involvement in blocking two Native American tribes from operating a casino near a MGM Resorts International gambling facility. In doing so, Rosen also prevented the Interior Department's Office of Inspector General from making a report about the casino deal public.

In February 2020, Rosen presented oral argument to the U.S. Supreme Court in a case involving prison inmate litigation (*Lomax v. Ortiz-Marquez*). The government prevailed in a unanimous opinion written by Justice Kagan.

Acting Attorney General

On December 14, 2020, it was announced that Rosen would become acting Attorney General ten days later, the day after William Barr's resignation took effect. According to a January 21, 2021 article in the *The New York Times*, even before Barr had left, Rosen was summoned to the Oval Office and pressured by President Donald Trump to aid him in his attempts to reverse the results of the 2020 election. Trump asked Rosen to file Justice Department legal briefs supporting lawsuits against the election results, and to appoint special prosecutors to investigate unfounded allegations of voter fraud and accusations against Dominion Voting Systems. Rosen declined, saying that the department had already investigated and had found no evidence of widespread voter fraud. However, Trump continued to press him and acting Deputy Attorney General Richard Donoghue.

In late December, Trump phoned Rosen "nearly every day" to tell him about claims of voter fraud or improper vote counts. Trump also asked Rosen to appoint a special counsel to look into allegations of voter fraud, and another special counsel to investigate Joe Biden's son Hunter.

In late December Jeffrey Clark, the acting head of the Justice Department's Civil Division, told Rosen and other top Justice Department officials that the Department should announce it was investigating serious election fraud issues. He asked them to sign a letter to Georgia officials claiming the DOJ had "identified significant concerns that may have impacted the outcome of the election in multiple States" and urging the Georgia legislature to convene a special session for the "purpose of considering issues pertaining to the appointment of Presidential Electors." Rosen and Donoghue rejected the proposal, as the Department had previously determined and announced that there was no significant fraud.

In early January, 2021 Clark reportedly met with Trump and suggested that he replace Rosen with Clark himself, who would then promote Trump's allegations of election fraud. Trump decided against removing Rosen only after learning that all the other Justice Department senior officials would resign if he did.

On January 6, 2021, in response to the attack on the United States Capitol, Rosen denounced the "intolerable attack on a fundamental institution of our democracy" and he urgently sent hundreds of DOJ law enforcement agents to the Capitol to help restore order, enabling Congress to complete its electoral vote certification that evening. Rosen also announced that DOJ would pursue investigations and criminal charges against the rioters, and approximately 150 were charged by the time he left DOJ two weeks later.

In testimony before Congress in May, 2021, Rosen said that "During my tenure, no special prosecutors were appointed, whether for election fraud or otherwise; no public statements were made questioning the election; no letters were sent to State officials seeking to overturn the election results; [and] no DOJ court actions or filings were submitted seeking to overturn election results." In early August, 2021, Rosen told the Justice Department inspector general and members of the Senate Judiciary Committee that Clark had tried to get the DOJ to help Trump subvert the election.

Jeffrey Rosen told the Justice Department Inspector General and congressional investigators that one of his deputies tried to help former President Donald J. Trump subvert the results of the 2020 election, according to a person familiar with the interviews.

Mr. Rosen had a two-hour meeting with the Justice Department's office of the Inspector General and provided closed-door testimony to the Senate Judiciary Committee.

The investigations were opened after a *New York Times* article that detailed efforts by Jeffrey Clark, the acting head of the Justice Department's civil division, to push top leaders to falsely and publicly assert that continuing election fraud investigations cast doubt on the Electoral College results. That prompted Mr. Trump to consider ousting Mr. Rosen and installing Mr. Clark at the top of the department to carry out that plan.

Mr. Trump never fired Mr. Rosen, but the plot highlights the former president's desire to batter the Justice Department into advancing his personal agenda. "Why don't you guys just seize [voting] machines?" Mr. Trump demanded to know at one point, later calling a top official at the Department of Homeland Security when informed that voting machines fell under that agency's purview, not the Justice Department's.

When top Justice Department officials repeatedly told him that they had investigated and debunked his allegations of widespread election fraud, Mr. Trump said they need not find evidence. "Just say the election is corrupt and leave the rest to me," he told them.

During a heated showdown in the Oval Office, only the threat of a mass resignation at the department persuaded Mr. Trump to back down. "He pressured the Justice Department to act as an arm of his re-election campaign," Representative Bennie Thompson, the Mississippi Democrat who is the chairman of the January 6th Committee, said of Mr. Trump. "He hoped law enforcement officials would give the appearance of legitimacy to his lies, so he and his allies had some veneer of credibility when they told the country that the election was stolen."

Conclusion

An independent Department of Justice and an elected Attorney General would remove the possibility of a future President of the United States making attempts to overturn an election with the assistance of the Justice Department. Trump's efforts to do this reinforce all the reasons for making the Justice Department immune from Presidential interference. President Trump and his Justice Department are the most important reason that we need an elected, independent Attorney General. Attorney General Bondi proves the point—she is acting only in President Trump's interests and at his command.

Chapter Eleven

How an Elected Attorney General Would Work

Under my proposal, the U.S. Attorney general would be elected every four years on the same ballot as candidates for President of the United States. Candidates for attorney general would seek their party's nomination state-by-state in primaries at the same time as the presidential primaries. This would not add any cost to these elections.

If a state, like Iowa, has a caucus system rather than a statewide ballot, each caucus would total the votes for candidates without any percentage minimum (Iowa presidential caucuses disallow candidates with less than 15% of a caucus vote. This would not be allowed concerning votes for the attorney general slot.)

Rather than electing delegates for candidates for attorney general, I propose that all votes be treated equally, and that the cumulative total of votes for each candidate would determine the nominee of the party. If there is not clear winner, the delegates at both parties national convention would choose between the two top candidates that were selected by the elections in all of the states and the District of Columbia.

Appointment of the FBI Director
and U.S. Attorneys

Currently, the President of the United States appoints the director of the Federal Bureau of Investigation and all 94 U.S. attorneys. Since the FBI director works under the U.S. Attorney General, I propose that the elected attorney general appoint the director of the Federal Bureau of Investigation for a term of ten years.

The U.S. Senate would be required to confirm this appointment.

To keep the Justice Department independent the attorney general should also appoint all the U.S. attorneys.

Chapter Twelve

Statute Creating Elected and Independent Attorney General

Congress passed the Judiciary Act of 1789 which established the Office of the Attorney General. The original duties of this officer were "to prosecute and conduct all suits in the Supreme Court in which the United States shall be concerned, and to give his advice and opinion upon questions of law when required by the President of the United States, or when requested by the heads of any of the departments." Judiciary Act of 1789, section 35. Currently, federal law provides that the President, with the advice and consent of the Senate, has the power to appoint the attorney general. 28 U.S.C. Section 503.

The Department of Justice was established in 1870 to support the Attorney General in the discharge of their responsibilities.

In 1966, Congress passed the text of 28 USC Section 532, codifying the early practice through which the Attorney General picks the FBI Director.

Congress reconsidered this approach just two years later, perhaps mindful that FBI Director J. Edgar Hoover would not in fact live forever and in any event appreciative that the FBI of the 1960s was a far more significant and independent organization than it had been when it started out as a small part of DOJ in the early 20th century. The Omnibus Crime Control and Safe Streets Act of 1968 included section 1101, which states:

> Effective as of the day following the date on which the present incumbent in the office of Director ceases to serve as such, the Director of the Federal Bureau of Investigation shall be appointed by the President, by and with the advice and consent of the Senate....

> 28 U.S. Code§ 541.United States attorneys (a) The President shall appoint, by and with the advice and consent of the Senate, a United

a. States attorney for each judicial district.

b. Each United States attorney shall be appointed for a term of four years. On the expiration of his term, a United States attorney shall continue to perform the duties of his office until his successor is appointed and qualifies.

c. Each United States attorney is subject to removal by the President. (Added Pub. L. 89–554, § 4(c), Sept. 6, 1966, 80 Stat. 617.)

I propose the Independent Attorney General Act as follows:

1. Every four years, on the same day that the election for president is held, the people of the United States shall vote for an attorney general.

2. The attorney general shall be elected by the popular vote of the voters of the United States.

3. The elected Attorney General shall be the director of the United States Department of Justice and shall appoint all of the inferior officers of the department, including all United States Attorneys and the Director of the Federal Bureau of Investigation. The

appointment of U.S. attorneys shall be confirmed by the United States Senate. The Director of the Federal Bureau of Investigation shall also be confirmed by the United States Senate.

4. The duty of the Attorney General shall be to protect the legal interests of the United States and its agencies, to advise agencies, and to warn agencies when he or she believes that they are acting contrary to law.

5. The Attorney General shall have the power to settle all claims and cases brought against the United States and to initiate civil and criminal cases in the interests of the United States.

About the Author

Joel D. Joseph is a lawyer who practiced law in the District of Columbia for most of his career. He is a graduate of Georgetown University Law Center. Joseph taught law at George Washington University.

He was a founder of the Special Prosecutor Project at George Washington University where he sought the appointment of special prosecutors in the Richard Nixon and Spiro Agnew cases.

Joseph has litigated against the United States Department of Justice in dozens of cases. One of the most prominent cases where he battled DOJ was the *Hungarian Gold Train* case, *Rosner v. United States*, 231 F. Supp. 2d 1202 (SD Fla. 2002). Joseph represented Hungarian survivors of the holocaust. They sued the United States because the U.S. Army seized their property from a train that contained millions of dollars of property stolen from Hungarian Jews by the Nazis. Joseph was disturbed that the Department of Justice would blindly represent the U.S. government no matter how abhorrent its behavior had been. Ultimately, however, the government settled and formally apologized to the Jewish community for its poor treatment of holocaust survivors. Most of the funds recovered were used to pay for medical care and senior living expenses for 10,000 Hungarian Jews who had survived when the case was settled.